★★★ A VISUAL HISTORY OF ★★★
WORLD MILITARY
MACHINES

Messerschmitt Bf 109G,
see page 122

★★★ A VISUAL HISTORY OF ★★★
WORLD MILITARY MACHINES

INCLUDES 1930–PRESENT

INSIDE THE WORLD'S MOST INCREDIBLE
COMBAT MACHINES

CONTRIBUTORS
Lieutenant Joshua S. Bettis, US Navy
Lieutenant Commander Josh Denning, US Navy
Major Alex Harris, UK Army Air Corps
JJ Molloy, Weapons Engineer

FOX CHAPEL
PUBLISHING

©2023 by Future Publishing Limited

Articles in this issue are translated or reproduced from *History of War Book of Combat Machines* and are the copyright of or licensed to Future Publishing Limited, a Future plc group company, UK 2022.

Used under license. All rights reserved. This version published by Fox Chapel Publishing Company, Inc., 903 Square Street, Mount Joy, PA 17552.

ISBN 978-1-4971-0401-3

Library of Congress Control Number: 2023936298

To learn more about the other great books from Fox Chapel Publishing, or to find a retailer near you, call toll-free 800-457-9112 or visit us at *www.FoxChapelPublishing.com*.

We are always looking for talented authors. To submit an idea, please send a brief inquiry to acquisitions@foxchapelpublishing.com.

Printed in Malaysia
First printing

★ ★ ★ WELCOME TO ★ ★ ★
A VISUAL HISTORY OF
WORLD MILITARY
MACHINES

Since the outbreak of the First World War more than 100 years ago, the technology powering the world's military forces has evolved at an unprecedented pace. The introduction of the first tanks during the Great War marked the start of an arms race that has continued to this day, and as we get our first glimpse at the next generation of military machines, it's incredible to think how far technology has come.

This book charts the history and development of these awesome military vehicles, from the fearsome German Tiger tanks of the Second World War, to the rise of the nuclear-powered submarine, to the high-tech fighter jets that now rule the skies across the globe. We'll show you all the facts and figures you need to become a combat machine expert, as well as breaking down each vehicle for an inside look at the technology that makes these tanks, choppers and battleships tick.

Read on to discover how the combat machines of today were made, and what the latest advances in technology will mean for warfare in the years to come.

CONTENTS

© BAE

© Thesupermat

WARSHIPS

68 Discover the battleships that rule the waves

WESTLAND WESSEX

142 The chopper that brought extra power to the battlefield

FIGHTER PLANES

110 Iconic aircraft from around the world

SEA

> "ADVANCEMENTS IN TECHNOLOGY COULD BRING BACK BATTLESHIP-LEVEL FIREPOWER, WITH ELECTROMAGNETIC RAILGUNS AND EVEN LASER WEAPONS"

AIR

20 GREATEST MACHINES OF WAR

From the AK-47 to the Apache gunship, the military weapons and vehicles of the last century have transformed modern warfare on land, sea and air

The machines of the 20th century were endlessly inventive and swung the pendulum for one side or another at crucial times. Just as a conflict looked as though it may grind to a stalemate, the order would be flipped on its head when a new invention made its timely debut on the battlefield.

The first machine guns brought about the end of marching in formation, while the arrival of the submarine blew the hierarchy of naval supremacy wide open. The most effective war machines are usually created as a response to seemingly unbeatable odds. The stealth bomber was invented to fight back against increasingly effective radar systems, while

tanks protected against the deadly machine gun fire that cut down infantry divisions in droves.

From the fall of once-great empires, to the first truly global conflicts and the rise of new superpowers, the last century produced increasingly effective and terrifying military technology. Listed here are just a few of the most devastating and revolutionary war machines that transformed the battlefields of one of history's bloodiest ever periods. Without the invention of these terrible but brilliant engineering marvels, the history of war would be very different indeed.

A stealth bomber on its first public flight in 1989. The B-2s cost a massive $135,000 per flight to operate

01 THE B-2 SPIRIT STEALTH BOMBER

IMAGINE AN AIRCRAFT ALMOST INVISIBLE TO RADAR THAT CAN STRIKE WITH EXPERT PRECISION FROM INCREDIBLY LONG RANGE. IT EXISTS, AND IT'S CALLED THE B-2

The world has come a long way since huge bombers blacked out the sky in the Second World War – now all you need is one. Among the most advanced of these bombers is undoubtedly the B-2 Spirit Stealth Bomber, which can reportedly do the job of 75 conventional aircraft. 21 of these modern aircraft were built (it would have been 132 if costs allowed) to strike heavily defended targets undetected.

An upgrade on the original Lockheed-Martin F-117 from 1981, its stealth is based on a smooth, contoured structure that keeps it partially hidden from radar. In addition, the bomber has systems that reduce its infrared, visual and electromagnetic visibility. A triumph of modern technology, underground bunkers can be struck by the craft's armaments and pilot error has been almost eliminated with the on-board computer, which also prevents stalls. All these features were put to deadly use over Kosovo in 1999 and Afghanistan in 2001, with precision attacks against munitions factories. Today the B-2 provides the USA with opportunity for lethal strikes.

Stealth bombers have the potential to reduce the size of air forces drastically due to their versatility and superior armament. Their presence in the latter days of the Cold War dissuaded the onset of full-scale war, as a single strike form a B-2 in retaliation would cause mass destruction. Its appeal to the US Air Force continues into the modern day, with the bombers set to receive a $9.9 billion upgrade.

TECHNICAL ASPECTS

COUNTRY OF ORIGIN: USA
FIRST PRODUCED: 1989
WINGSPAN: 172FT
RANGE: 6,000MI
TOP SPEED: HIGH SUBSONIC
WEAPONRY: NUCLEAR WARHEADS, ADVANCED CRUISE MISSILES, MARK-84 BOMBS

KEY TECHNOLOGY

The advent of fully working military radar systems during the Second World War marked the need for stealth technology. The B-2 makes itself only partially invisible to radar, as its unique design is excellent at reflecting signals at a different angle, rather than straight back to its receiver. Additionally, the dark color absorbs high amounts of light, while the tiny iron spheres used on its surface paint dissipate the radar energy as heat, so only miniscule amounts make it back to the radio transmitter.

Design, shape and even texture helps B-2s avoid detection in a way that no craft has done before

02 MARK I TANK

THE FIRST TANK TO EVER SEE BATTLE CHANGED CONFLICT FOREVER, HELPING ELIMINATE THE STALEMATE OF TRENCH WARFARE

Only 250 of these metal beasts were created and even less saw battle on the muddy Western Front, but the Mark I signalled the dawn of a new type of warfare. With the stalemate of the trenches wearing down both sides in World War One, the tank was designed to be used as an armored battering ram that could tear down enemy fortifications.

'Male' tanks were armed with three machine guns and one quarter-pounder gun, while the lighter 'female' versions contained six machine guns but less armor. The guns on the sides of this behemoth would mow down any infantry that would dare cross its path – at least that was the theory.

In its first few engagements, the Mark I regularly overheated and broke down and many were captured by the Imperial German Army. Conditions inside the tank were almost unbearable, with temperatures reaching 122 degrees Fahrenheit and the loud machinery almost deafening.

As the war continued, improved versions were put into production, such as the Mark IV, which had tougher armor and better weaponry

TECHNICAL ASPECTS

COUNTRY OF ORIGIN: GREAT BRITAIN
FIRST PRODUCED: 1916
LENGTH: 32FT
WEIGHT: 28 TONS
TOP SPEED: 3.2MPH
WEAPONRY: TWO SIX-POUNDER (57MM) GUNS AND TWO AIR-COOLED MACHINE GUNS

ARMOR
One of the Mark I's biggest flaws was its structure. The armor was bulletproof but was prone to splitting the projectiles fired at the tank into shrapnel, which could injure the crew. In early models the tank crew were compelled to wear chain mail!

CREW
An eight-man crew would work inside a Mark I tank. Effective teamwork was difficult as the lack of light meant during battle the interior was in almost complete darkness. The excruciating noise meant that tactics and strategy were often incoherent

ENGINE
The engine of choice in the tank was a water-cooled 105hp. Due to the vehicle's bulk, this power was simply not enough and the Mark I was often reduced to a crawl as it was overtaken by infantry

DESIGN
An unusual shape enabled the tracks of the tanks to be as long as possible. The prototype for the Mark I, Little Willie, was deemed neither long nor strong enough to tackle trenches, so a rhombus was deemed effective

WHEELS AND ROOF
Unlike later models, the Mark I had both extra wheels and a sloped roof. The wheels were intended to aid steering, while the roof could deflect grenades. Both of these features were quickly phased out in later models

HEAVY TANKS OF WORLD WAR ONE FROM THE MARK I TO THE MARK X

1915	April 1916	August 1916	March 1917	May 1917	July 1917	November 1917	April 1918	September 1918	1919
'Little Wille' is tested as the first prototype of the Mark I – the precursor to all tanks.	150 Mark I tanks are ordered to be built for the war in the trenches.	The first batch of Mark I tanks make their debut just in time for the Somme offensive.	The first Mark II tanks enter the fray, ready made with improvements over the original model.	The vastly improved Mark IV is introduced onto the Western Front after the Mark III is used purely for training purposes.	The new Mark VII is born after co-development with the USA. The VI had previously been canceled after disagreements arose during production.	476 tanks do battle at Cambrai and make significant advances into German territory across the Hindenburg Line.	The first ever tank-to-tank battle sees Mark IVs combat German A7Vs.	The Mark VIII is created after a joint project between the USA, Britain and France and remains in use until 1934.	The last two 'Mark' models are created, with the IX a troop carrier. The X never makes it off the production line.

"TANKS STILL PLAY A MAJOR PART IN CONFLICTS ACROSS THE GLOBE – THE MARK I IS WHERE THEY ALL BEGAN"

The potential was seen in the Mark I though, so later versions of the tank would succeed where it failed. After small advances in the II and III, the Mark IV was a vastly improved machine. Containing much thicker armor and a better engine, this would have the greatest impact on the Western Front, with its successor only available in the latter stages of the war.

The tank became the new cavalry of the battlefield, and the various 'Mark' models played a big part in the emergence of tank dominance. The Mark IX was the final tank of the line to be built, but the design was still used after the Great War. Mark Vs were used by both sides in the Russian Civil War and two were even found in the Battle of Berlin in the last days of the Third Reich.

Although initially unreliable, these tanks were pioneers for modern warfare. During the Battle of Kursk in 1943 over 6,000 tanks duked it out on the battlefield. The Nazi blitzkrieg would have stalled without them, and during the post-World War years, tanks still play a major part in conflicts across the globe – the Mark I is where they all began.

The tank was a steep learning curve, so it included many different features, such as back wheels and extra roof protection

IN ACTION
THE BATTLE OF CAMBRAI: GIANT STEPS IN CATERPILLAR TRACKS

By late 1917 the role of tanks was increasing after many failed attempts to incorporate the mechanical monster in warfare. After struggling in the mud pits of the Somme, the dry plains of Cambrai were ideal for tank tracks.

The attack began on the morning of the 20 November as 476 of the machines advanced on German positions. The surprise attack was a resounding success, with German forces pushed back by 3.7 miles (6km) as the Hindenburg Line was breached for the first time during the war. On the first day alone, 8,000 prisoners and 100 guns were taken. However, a German counterattack nullified a sizeable portion of the British gains, as the deployment of tanks didn't quite wear down the German resistance completely. Nonetheless, the effectiveness of tanks had finally been proved and it was from here on out that the machine became an essential instrument of war.

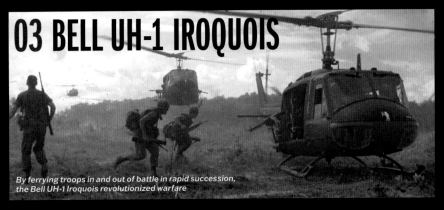

03 BELL UH-1 IROQUOIS

By ferrying troops in and out of battle in rapid succession, the Bell UH-1 Iroquois revolutionized warfare

Nicknamed the Huey, this popular vehicle machine was vital for the deployment of American troops during the Vietnam War. Powered by a jet turbine that had never been installed on a helicopter before, 16,000 of these small vehicles were made and are still in use by the US Drug Enforcement Agency (DEA).

These multipurpose helicopters could ferry up to 14 soldiers to and from battlefields. M-240 and Browning guns could also be attached.

04 TIGER II

The Tiger II was beset by manufacturing issues after being rushed off the Third Reich production line in an attempt to save the war

One of the deadliest tanks of the entire Second World War, the Tiger II would have dominated the battlefield if it weren't for its inherent production flaws. Feared by the Allied forces, this armored beast quickly earned an aura of invincibility because of its thick armor and deadly 88mm turret gun. After the war, German Tiger II technology and prototypes were used for the future tanks of the 20th century.

05 C-130 HERCULES

The C-130 is used in a variety of missions, from cargo drops, to humanitarian efforts to troop deployment

Since its first flight in 1955, there hasn't been a military aircraft quite as reliable and adaptable as the Hercules. Currently operated by over 16 countries, the C-130 can carry various payloads up to over 20,000kg.

Capable of operating over a range of 3,800km, it also fulfils the role of a long-distance cargo and transport aircraft perfectly, and there's still seemingly no need to replace it, even after 60 years in service.

06 M1 ABRAMS MEDIUM BATTLE TANK

A VETERAN OF WARS ALL OVER THE GLOBE SINCE 1979, THIS MACHINE HELPED SHUNT ARMORED GROUND WARFARE INTO THE MODERN ERA

The M1 Abrams battle tank was born after many failed attempts by the USA and Germany to create a tank to rival the Soviet T-72. By 1979 the US had decided to go solo and the outcome was the M1 Abrams, which excels in the three key areas of tank warfare: firepower, protection and mobility. It was produced six years after the Yom Kippur War, which saw the largest tank battle since the Second World War. An all-weather vehicle, it still plays a major role in the US Army, with the ability to go head-to-head with other armored vehicles, while providing infantry support and mobile firepower.

It served during the Gulf War, in Afghanistan and the 2003 invasion of Iraq. In all these conflicts the Abrams outclassed its rivals with superior range, night vision and thermal sight capabilities.

Only nine were put beyond repair in the whole of the Gulf War and the tank was essential to the success of Operation Desert Storm. Nearly 9,000 have been constructed for use worldwide and it's still in production after 35 years. Many have described it as being the first US tank to outclass its Soviet equivalent and many variants on the original design have been made due to its success. The model M1A2 is undoubtedly the most advanced tank operating in the world today.

Above: With tough armor all over, the M1 Abrams is highly resistant to most gun and missile fire

Below: The power of the Abrams' 105mm main gun has been upgraded to a 120mm version on the M1A1 and M1A2

KEY TECHNOLOGY

A tough duo of rolled homogeneous steel plates and Chobham laminate keep the tank and its crew well protected. Neither HEAT warheads nor Sabot rounds can puncture the inner layer of the tank and the structure also prevents injury by having armored storage for the tank's own armaments. Better still, and much more inconspicuous, is an air-purification system dedicated to repelling biological attack.

TECHNICAL ASPECTS

COUNTRY OF ORIGIN: USA

FIRST PRODUCED: 1979

LENGTH: 32.25FT

WEIGHT: 139,080LB

TOP SPEED: 42MPH

WEAPONRY: 120MM MAIN GUN, 12.7MM BROWNING M1HB ANTI-AIRCRAFT HEAVY MACHINE GUN, 2X 7.62MM M240 MACHINE GUNS, 2X 6 SMOKE GRENADE DISCHARGES

07 AK-47 ASSAULT RIFLE

A COMBINATION OF A SUBMACHINE GUN'S FIREPOWER, WITH ALL THE ACCURACY OF A RIFLE

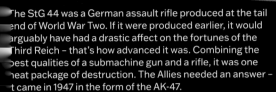

The distinctive curved magazine of the AK-47 is a common sight, with an estimated 100 million having been manufactured

The StG 44 was a German assault rifle produced at the tail end of World War Two. If it were produced earlier, it would arguably have had a drastic affect on the fortunes of the Third Reich – that's how advanced it was. Combining the best qualities of a submachine gun and a rifle, it was one neat package of destruction. The Allies needed an answer – it came in 1947 in the form of the AK-47.

Created in the USSR by inventor and engineer Mikhail Kalashnikov, the weapon's ability to fire intermediate power cartridges at a rapid rate put it head and shoulders above the competition and paved the way for a wave of assault rifles such as the M16 and FAMAS.

It saw widespread action in the Korean War and was only upstaged in the Russian military by the mid-1970s with the development of the AK-74. There have even been stories that during the Vietnam War, US GIs stole AK-47s from the Viet Cong as they were still superior to the American equivalents. Currently, it's the weapon of choice for militant groups the world over due to its low cost and general all-round effectiveness. More AK rifles have been produced than all the other assault rifles combined and it remains a key player in warfare.

KEY TECHNOLOGY

The AK-47 was a phenomenon in so many ways and raised the bar in land warfare. The next stage of assault rifle evolution after the StG 44 took the first steps – its selective fire enabled it to be used in all areas of war, from street-to-street skirmishes to raids on fortified positions. An incredibly basic weapon for all its advances, the rifle only weighs nine pounds. It can be stripped and cleaned in under a minute, making it invaluable for tense battlefield situations.

TECHNICAL ASPECTS

COUNTRY OF ORIGIN: SOVIET UNION
FIRST PRODUCED: 1947
LENGTH: 35IN
ACTION: GAS-PERATED ROTATING B
RANGE: 1310FT
AMMUNITION: 7.62X39MM ROUNDS

08 THE BLACKBIRD

Originally kept under wraps as a US and UK secret Black Project, the Lockheed SR-71 Blackbird was a technological wonder. The fastest plane of all time (reaching an eye-melting 2,193mph, it was also one of the highest-flying military aircraft ever made. The plane was so fast, it even broke both the sound and heat barriers and required a specialist fuel and titanium structure to fly.

Devised after the U2 incident in 1960, the Blackbird demonstrated that the US needed a quicker and higher-flying reconnaissance aircraft that couldn't be tracked by the USSR. The designers of the Blackbird described it as their hardest ever assignment, as the plane was so different and advanced compared with anything that came before. 32 were constructed in total and served as scouting aircraft for over 30 years. The details of a vast majority of these missions are still classified.

The altitude and speed of the Blackbird meant pilots were forced to wear astronaut-like suits that protected them from the elements

09 ENIGMA MACHINE

Highly sophisticated devices for their time, Enigma machines held the key to many of the Wehrmacht's secrets. An electro-mechanical rotor cipher machine, the device was used by the Third Reich to transport and receive covert messages and tactics without the risk of being decoded.

Capable of millions of combinations, the Allies captured many of these messages but were only able to break the code in 1940 with the help of Polish experts from the Government Code and Cypher School (GC&CS) in Bletchley Park, England. The code was eventually broken by using a device called a Bombe, which could attempt hundreds of potential codes per minute until it found the correct combination.

It has been speculated that this breakthrough shortened the war by up to two years, such was the effectiveness and importance of the machine.

The Enigma machine was so effective, British agents had to play down their successes so the Axis powers didn't get wind of their discovery

10 AH-64 APACHE ATTACK HELICOPTER

THIS HELICOPTER GUNSHIP IS THE TANK'S WORST ENEMY AND CAN ELIMINATE VAST SWATHS OF HEAVY INFANTRY IN SECONDS

Since their inception in the late 20th century, advanced attack helicopters have been a nightmare for troops both on land and at sea – the most notable of these is the AH-64 Apache.

Prior to attack helicopters, infantry could advance along territory, with infrequent air strikes from bombers being their only airborne concern. Now, with a chain-gun-equipped helicopter prowling the skies, tactics and strategies have become very different. The AH-64 can be assigned to almost any mission, from destroying fortifications, to delaying and disrupting the movement of troops. It's even more dangerous at night, with the help of Target Acquisition Designation Sight (TADS) and Pilot Night Vision Sensors (PNVS).

The gunship's M230 chain gun can strafe and lay waste to infantry, while Hellfire missiles can take down armored vehicles, ships and structures. If the Apache is threatened from the air, its Hydra rockets will combat most aerial rivals. The US Army has ordered over 800 of the machines since they were first introduced, while others have found their way into the Israeli and Egyptian air forces. The advanced attack helicopter reached its zenith in Operation Desert Storm, where it was used to decimate 500 Iraqi tanks and other armored vehicles.

Apaches have a rapid response rate to enemy threats, and can be deployed far quicker than land-based vehicles. Additionally, the gunship requires far less space and fewer resources than fighter jets. The AH-64 can also be called upon in all manner of inhospitable conditions.

Naturally, various methods have been devised to combat the attack helicopter, and militants that come into contact with the Apache now carry rocket-propelled grenades.

The AH-64 has the ability to hover in wait and then unleash Hellfire and Hydra missiles to eliminate targets

TECHNICAL ASPECTS

COUNTRY OF ORIGIN: USA
FIRST PRODUCED: 1983
LENGTH: 58.17FT
WEIGHT: 16,027LB
TOP SPEED: 170MPH
WEAPONRY: HELLFIRE LASER-DESIGNATED MISSILES, M230 CHAIN GUN, HYDRA ROCKETS

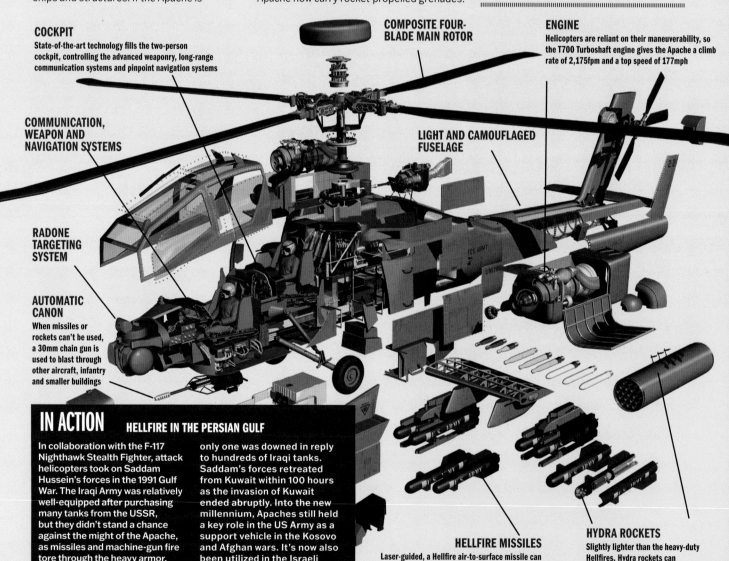

COCKPIT
State-of-the-art technology fills the two-person cockpit, controlling the advanced weaponry, long-range communication systems and pinpoint navigation systems

COMPOSITE FOUR-BLADE MAIN ROTOR

ENGINE
Helicopters are reliant on their maneuverability, so the T700 Turboshaft engine gives the Apache a climb rate of 2,175fpm and a top speed of 177mph

COMMUNICATION, WEAPON AND NAVIGATION SYSTEMS

LIGHT AND CAMOUFLAGED FUSELAGE

RADONE TARGETING SYSTEM

AUTOMATIC CANON
When missiles or rockets can't be used, a 30mm chain gun is used to blast through other aircraft, infantry and smaller buildings

HELLFIRE MISSILES
Laser-guided, a Hellfire air-to-surface missile can rip through armored vehicles and bunkers with ease. They are particularly effective against tanks

HYDRA ROCKETS
Slightly lighter than the heavy-duty Hellfires, Hydra rockets can be used against other aircraft or smaller ground targets

IN ACTION | HELLFIRE IN THE PERSIAN GULF

In collaboration with the F-117 Nighthawk Stealth Fighter, attack helicopters took on Saddam Hussein's forces in the 1991 Gulf War. The Iraqi Army was relatively well-equipped after purchasing many tanks from the USSR, but they didn't stand a chance against the might of the Apache, as missiles and machine-gun fire tore through the heavy armor. They were so successful that only one was downed in reply to hundreds of Iraqi tanks. Saddam's forces retreated from Kuwait within 100 hours as the invasion of Kuwait ended abruptly. Into the new millennium, Apaches still held a key role in the US Army as a support vehicle in the Kosovo and Afghan wars. It's now also been utilized in the Israeli Army.

FLYING ON THE FRONTLINE

MAJOR ALEX HARRIS OF THE UK ARMY AIR CORPS SHARES HIS EXPERIENCES OF FLYING APACHE AIRCRAFT

HOW LONG DOES IT TAKE TO TRAIN TO FLY AN APACHE? IS IT INITIALLY DIFFICULT TO HANDLE?

You first have to complete the army pilot's course, which is modular and takes about two years. Once you have been awarded your army flying wings you might get selected to train on the Apache. The first part is called Conversion to Type (CTT), which teaches you how to fly the aircraft and lasts about six months. If successful, you move on to the next phase which is called Conversion to Role (CTR). This teaches you how to fly the aircraft in all scenarios and also lasts six months.

The culmination is the live firing of all the Apache weapon types in Arizona, USA. You are then a qualified Apache pilot. Even after all of that, you are constantly learning and attending different courses. These could be such things as learning to operate from a Royal Navy ship, or becoming a weapons instructor. Initially it can be quite difficult to fly, as it's much larger and more complex than the training aircraft.

The courses are all progressive though and you can't advance until you have mastered the basics. The aircraft has a very good stabilization system to ensure that it's a steady platform from which to launch weapons, so when these are working for you it is a great aircraft to fly.

WHAT WAS THE APACHE'S ROLE IN THE THEATERS YOU FLEW IN AND HOW EFFECTIVE WAS IT?

Its main role was to support the ground forces with precision weapons when they got engaged by the Taliban and were pinned down. With a talk on over the radio from the ground forces, the Apaches were able to identify the enemy, single them out from the population and built-up areas, before decisively engaging them.

We also escorted the Chinooks that carried the Medical Emergency Response Team (MERT). This life-saving asset often picked up seriously wounded casualties from the battlefield while the firefight still went on around them. They were a big target for the Taliban and it was our job to try and destroy the enemy before they could engage them.

DOES THE HELICOPTER FORM PART OF A SQUAD OR IS IT FLOWN SOLO WHEN ON THE ATTACK?

Although they can work alone, Apaches would normally work as a pair. This is known as a Flight. During an engagement one aircraft would act as the shooter and the other as the looker. This means that while one is zoomed in on the target, the other aircraft is looking out wider for more targets in depth.

The looker will also put himself in a position to follow up on the first aircraft's attack if necessary. If the Squadron is fighting together you may find two or more Flights working in an engagement area to prosecute targets.

HOW DOES YOUR CO-PILOT ASSIST YOU?

While the Co-Pilot Gunner is heads-down in the sight looking for enemy, the pilot is looking after the safety of the aircraft. He is monitoring the systems and ensuring that all is as it should be, but more than that he is watching for any close-in enemy trying to shoot them down. With the Helmet Mounted Display, the pilot is only a couple of button presses away from firing the 30mm. It can be slaved to his head position so that wherever he looks, all he has to do is pull the trigger and he is firing on-target.

HAVE YOU EVER HAD TO MAKE A EMERGENCY LANDING?

In Afghanistan on Very High Readiness (VHR) we got a call to go and support some ground forces who were under fire. However, not long after take off, one of our two engines developed a serious fault and started to break up, so we had to shut it down. Because of the weight of the weapons we had on board and the fact that our performance was low in the hot and high conditions, we were unable to maintain level flight and so started to descend to the desert floor.

We worked out that we could just about make it back to Camp Bastion before we would hit the deck, so we nursed it back to the Apache landing strip, landed on and parked up. We jumped straight out of that one and moved our kit into the aircraft next to it, getting back out in under five minutes. We eventually got to the site of the battle and were engaging with Hellfire missiles and 30mm within minutes of arriving.

WHAT WAS YOUR MOST MEMORABLE FLIGHT?

Probably the first time I ever fired the weapons in a combat situation. We were fighting in the middle of a city and some enemy armed with heavy weapons and suicide vests had taken over the top two floors of a hotel that overlooked a friendly camp. They were firing down into the camp and causing friendly casualties. We arrived not long after it began and I remember thinking that if I got this wrong in such a built-up area, then the consequences could be terrible. However, the training soon kicked in and operating as a crew and as a Flight, we successfully defeated the enemy. I do remember afterwards that the hotel had some serious holes in it and I'd have some explaining to do when I got back to base.

11
HMS DREADNOUGHT

THE DAWN OF THE FIRST DREADNOUGHT BATTLESHIP REVOLUTIONIZED NAVAL WARFARE PRIOR TO TWO WORLD WARS

If there's one war machine that demonstrated the intensity of the Anglo-German arms race, it was the Dreadnought class of battleship. The first, HMS Dreadnought, was completed in 1906 and completely eclipsed what came before. With its steam turbine powerplant, it could roar through the waves at high speeds while aiming the most heavily-armed naval guns in history at an enemy vessel. It was the first vessel to focus entirely on 'big gun' armament, which had a range of a massive 14.2 miles. The guns were controlled by all-new electronic transmitting equipment that could aim the artillery incredibly accurately for the time.

Dreadnought was even the first ship to house the captain and officers nearer the bridge at the front, unlike the old style seen on tall ships in the age of sail. With such advanced armament and technology, the design became immensely popular and by 1914 the Royal Navy had constructed 19, while the Imperial German Navy had 13 in its fleet. The impact was so great that only a year later 'Super-Dreadnoughts' were being produced. The Dreadnought class had revolutionized the war at sea and a constant stream of updated models would follow right up until the height of the Cold War, when nuclear submarines began to change naval combat once again.

TECHNICAL ASPECTS

COUNTRY OF ORIGIN: GREAT BRITAIN
FIRST PRODUCED: 1906
LENGTH: 525FT
WEIGHT: 20,282 TONS
TOP SPEED: 21 KNOTS (24MPH)
WEAPONRY: TEN 305MM GUNS, 24 76MM GUNS, FIVE TORPEDO TUBES

KEY TECHNOLOGY

Without the steam turbine, the Dreadnought class of battleships would have not been the significant machine it was. The innovative technology was a British invention from 1884, but this was the first time it would be used on a warship. The system replaced the triple-expansion engine that had been used so extensively in older ships and made the HMS Dreadnought the fastest battleship in the world. With the new mechanism, the battleship now had a range of approx 7,620 miles.

The Minigun enabled a weapon with the power of the M61 Vulcan to be used on ships, turrets and armored vehicles

12 M61 VULCAN

THE GATLING GUN OF THE MODERN ERA, THE M61 VULCAN SHOWCASES THE TRUE POWER OF CONTEMPORARY HAND-OPERATED WEAPONS

A gigantic weapon of war, the M61 Vulcan was initially devised as an anti-aircraft gun. Its rotating six-bolt barrel gives it a much higher rate of fire and reliability than single-barrel machine guns, which would overheat after persistent use.

An ammo belt was originally used to feed the bullet-hungry firearm, but after a jamming problem the belts were replaced by a linkless feed system. The gun is powered both hydraulically and electrically by aircraft and can fire both incendiary and armor-piercing rounds. The invention of the weapon gave fighter jets an alternative to using missiles at short range and has one of the highest firing rates of any machine gun. The M61 has also been used on the ground as an air defence system in armored vehicles and its successor, the M134 Minigun, was used in helicopters as a response to RPG fire from the ground.

The M134 has made the weapon class much more effective, as it can be placed on gun emplacements. This scaled-down version of the original made the weapon more readily transportable but with a decreased rate of fire. Despite its inability to be carried and fired by a single infantryman (as is often the myth), the M61 Vulcan has made all types of military aircraft much more resistant to ground fire and more effective at taking out ground units. Its high rate of fire means successful hits are achievable even at jet speeds.

TECHNICAL ASPECTS

COUNTRY OF ORIGIN: USA
FIRST PRODUCED: 1959
LENGTH: 72IN
ACTION: HYDRAULICALLY OPERATED BELT-FED UNIT
RATE OF FIRE: 6,000 ROUNDS PER MINUTE
AMMUNITION: 20X102MM ROUNDS

KEY TECHNOLOGY

Overheating was always an issue with machine guns with a high rate of fire, but the M61 Vulcan managed to remedy this downside. By using six separate barrels firing 1,000 rounds a minute, none of the systems would overheat or malfunction but 6,000 rounds of ammunition would still be fired off in a minute's worth of firing. This was extremely useful on military aircraft where a fault could not be fixed mid-flight.

B-52 STRATOFORTRESS

This gigantic bomber was one of the biggest and most-powerful aircraft ever made. Powered by eight engines, its original purpose was to carry atomic bombs behind the Iron Curtain if relations with the Soviet Union soured. Thankfully, it never had the opportunity to deploy its one-megaton nuclear warhead, so it was confined to bombing missions using conventional munitions.

It proved to be very versatile plane, carrying up to 60,000lbs of bombs ranging from nuclear to precision-guided cruise missiles. The B-52 was hugely effective during Vietnam and the Gulf Wars and its descendants have been in frequent use in Iraq and the Balkans. The plane's sheer bulk means that the B-52 is also used as a carrier for air rocket launches. The success of this war machine has meant that it's now the longest-serving bomber in US military history and is set to remain in operation until 2040.

The B-52 is an exceptional air launcher. Here it is (inset) carrying two Lockheed D-21 reconnaissance drones

14 HUMVEE

The HUMVEE saw widespread use in the Gulf War and has become and integral part of the US Army since

After the Vietnam War, the aging US M151 Jeep was in drastic need of an upgrade. The result finally came in the early 1980s, when the High Mobility Multipurpose Wheeled Vehicle (HMMWV/HUMVEE) was developed.

Designed as an infantry support vehicle, the HUMVEE features great all-round capabilities and could even be dropped into battle from the air. Lightweight and four-wheel drive, the vehicle is highly flexible and can perform a variety of battlefield and reconnaissance roles. It provides an essential middle ground between surveillance and the heavy artillery rolling in.

A HUMVEE can carry a variety of equipment, from machine guns to missile launchers, and so can also act as a store for weaponry and ammunition. Since its inception there have been numerous improvements on the original design, and the vehicle has subsequently become a staple of the US Army.

15 USS NAUTILUS (SSN-571)

In the post-World War era, nuclear power was blazing its way into many naval propulsion systems, providing extra power, speed and range. The first to embrace this new power source was the USS Nautilus (SSN-571), the first nuclear submarine completed in 1955.

With this new power cell, submarines could theoretically spend unlimited amounts of time underwater, a feature that would become imperative in the Cold War. The USSR's first nuclear sub, the K-3, followed hot on the heels of the Nautilus in 1958, but could only watch as its rival smash every submerged speed and distance record.

The nuclear age had begun, so US and Soviet submarines would closely monitor one another for the remainder of the war. The influence of the Nautilus can be seen today in the Trident UK nuclear deterrent system and the legions of submarines that still patrol the depths.

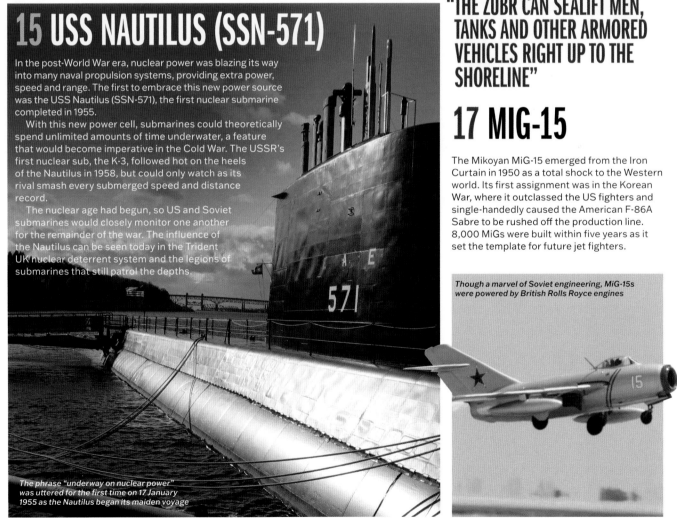

The phrase "underway on nuclear power" was uttered for the first time on 17 January 1955 as the Nautilus began its maiden voyage

16 ZUBR-CLASS LCAC MILITARY HOVERCRAFT

The largest class of military hovercraft in the world is the Zubr, which became an important part of warfare after its inception in 1988. Providing the same role that transport helicopters do for ground troops, the Zubr can sealift men, tanks and other armored vehicles right up to the shoreline in coastal assaults.

There are currently nine in this class of military hovercraft in active service within the Russian, Ukrainian and Greek navies

"THE ZUBR CAN SEALIFT MEN, TANKS AND OTHER ARMORED VEHICLES RIGHT UP TO THE SHORELINE"

17 MIG-15

The Mikoyan MiG-15 emerged from the Iron Curtain in 1950 as a total shock to the Western world. Its first assignment was in the Korean War, where it outclassed the US fighters and single-handedly caused the American F-86A Sabre to be rushed off the production line. 8,000 MiGs were built within five years as it set the template for future jet fighters.

Though a marvel of Soviet engineering, MiG-15s were powered by British Rolls Royce engines

A specialized Machine Gun Corps was created in 1915 to give the weapon a higher status in the British army

IN ACTION

THE SOMME MACHINE-GUN MASSACRE

With more than a million men killed, the 1916 Battle of the Somme is believed to be one of the bloodiest battles in human history. This was partly down to the lack of tactics to combat the new weapon of the generation, the machine gun. Unaware of the awesome power of the weapon, both sides were sitting ducks when wading through the thick mud against a wall of bullets. Reports suggested that Vickers guns alone fired in excess of a million rounds over a 12-hour period. Originally used as a defensive battlefield support weapon, the Battle of the Somme showed just how devastating machine-gun fire could be when used in an offensive capacity. With the stalemate of trench warfare ending, it was imperative that machine guns became lighter and more compact. This led to the invention of lighter machine guns and, latterly, assault rifles.

18 VICKERS MK1

DEVELOPED IN THE EARLY 20TH CENTURY, THIS MACHINE GUN WOULD REVOLUTIONIZE THE WAY BATTLES WERE FOUGHT AND HOW ARMIES WERE TRAINED

It may not have been the first machine gun, but the Vickers MK 1 was essential to the rapid changes in warfare at the start of the century. Both the Gatling and Maxim guns preceded it, but its development in 1912 saw the Vickers become the most reliable and versatile machine gun of its day. By using a water-cooling jacket around the barrel, it could fire off rounds more accurately and quicker than ever before. The wall of bullets spelled the end for infantry formations and accelerated the beginning of trench warfare and no-man's land. Huge pitched battles with massive assembled infantry divisions would be no more.

Weighing in at 44 pounds, the gun would be placed in a hidden position and fired on unsuspecting foes. Its bulk meant it had to be static to be effective, but in such a slow-moving conflict, this wasn't a problem.

However, it was more than just a gun – the Vickers would contain a water-condensing can and hose, a wooden sight, ammunition box and a canvas jacket. All this would be operated by a crew of up to six soldiers. Without a water supply (one batch would evaporate after 750 rounds had been fired), it would quickly overheat, so gas-powered machine guns soon became preferred.

The Vickers's counterparts in the field of battle were the German MG08 and French Hotchkiss. The gun was so popular that 12 were being made every week for the British Army and 39,473 were in use by 1918. The

Vickers Company even had to lower its price to £80 per gun, so the government could finance the demand. In fact, the guns proved to be even more versatile than first thought and, armed with an interrupter gear, were attached to the fighters of the Royal Flying Corps. The fighters were now able to take on the Imperial German Air Force in ever-deadlier dogfights.

As the Great War wore on, the Vickers was slowly phased out by the Lewis gun, which boasted improved reliability and accuracy. However, the Vickers name did make a comeback with later gas-operated models lasting up to the Second World War. In fact, the British Army only considered the weapon completely obsolete in the late 1960s. The gun was an important template for later

TECHNICAL ASPECTS

COUNTRY OF ORIGIN: GREAT BRITAIN
FIRST PRODUCED: 1912
LENGTH: 38.5IN
CALIBER: .303IN
RATE OF FIRE: 450-550 ROUNDS PER MINUTE
FIRING RANGE: 13,451FT

weapons, such as the MG32 and Browning, and was the first to successfully work on and improve the Maxim gun. Warfare has never been the same since.

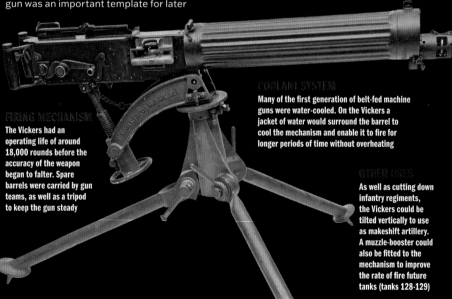

FIRING MECHANISM

The Vickers had an operating life of around 18,000 rounds before the accuracy of the weapon began to falter. Spare barrels were carried by gun teams, as well as a tripod to keep the gun steady

COOLANT SYSTEM

Many of the first generation of belt-fed machine guns were water-cooled. On the Vickers a jacket of water would surround the barrel to cool the mechanism and enable it to fire for longer periods of time without overheating

OTHER USES

As well as cutting down infantry regiments, the Vickers could be tilted vertically to use as makeshift artillery. A muzzle-booster could also be fitted to the mechanism to improve the rate of fire future tanks (tanks 128-129)

MACHINE GUN LEGACY

THE VICKERS' RIVALS AND THE GUNS IT WOULD INFLUENCE

MG08

The German machine gun of choice in the First World War, the Maschinegewehr 08 was very similar to the slightly older British Maxim gun. At its peak, over 14,000 were being churned out of German factories every month and it was upgraded to an air-cooled model in 1918.

HOTCHKISS

The most cumbersome of all the WWI machine guns, the French Hotchkiss had a lower fire rate than the MG08 and Vickers. As the war went on, the French switched to using the Chauchat light machine gun as more mobile firearms became preferable.

LEWIS GUN

Used by the British in the Great War, the Lewis gun used a circular magazine rather than a belt-fed mechanism. This highly effective weapon was nicknamed the 'Belgian Rattlesnake' by the Germans and was used in unison with the Vickers. It began to phase the Vickers out as it was discovered that six could be made in the time that one Vickers could.

MG34

The MG34 was one of the most versatile of the post-Vickers guns. The Wehrmacht created the Maschinegewher 34 so it could be used on a bipod, a tripod or even without a mount. Effective and powerful, it was replaced by the MG42, which is considered once of the best machine guns of all time.

M1917 BROWNING

Perhaps the longest serving of all machine guns of the era, the M1917 was used from World War One right up until the Vietnam War. It was designed by the USA and signified their development as a military power, as before the Browning, their machine guns were very out-dated compared to the European equivalents.

Flamethrowers are unstable weapons of war, but there aren't many war machines that inspire as much terror

19 FLAMETHROWER

The turn of the 20th Century signalled the dawn of a devastating new weapon in warfare: the modern flamethrower. Yet another war machine devised to end the horrors of trench warfare, the flamethrower first saw battle on the Western Front as both sides attempted to flush out enemy trenches.

The original weapon was operated by two men and had a range of up to 131 feet, however, they had limited usage as they only had enough oil for 40-second bursts. Flamethrowers were later installed on tanks in the Second World War and were highly effective as a shock weapon. The armored protection negated the weapon's lengthy reload times and a tank could store additional fuel to reload. Due to their inconsistent nature, flamethrowers have been gradually phased out of military use, but are still readily used by militant groups. These shocking weapons have encouraged the use of other incendiary weapons such as napalm and thermobaric bombs.

20 USS ENTERPRISE (CVN 65)

In 1962 a new supercarrier was born that would be the first nuclear-powered aircraft carrier ever built. Made of nearly 100,000 tons of metal, the USS Enterprise could carry over 60 aircraft and represented a new dawn for seagoing air bases.

Powered by eight reactors, it was thrust into action almost immediately, as it participated in the blockade on Cuba in the wake of the 1962 Cuban Missile Crisis. In 1965 it became the first nuclear-powered ship to engage in conflict as it entered the Vietnam War to provide support for the frontline troops. Nicknamed 'Big E', she is still the longest naval vessel in the world and has opened up a whole new era for supercarriers. The major carriers since include the entire Nimitz class of carrier and the forthcoming USS Gerald R Ford ship.

The Enterprise is a fully-functioning floating battlestation with a 4.5-acre flight deck and a 3.5-acre hangar

Alamy, DK Images; Corbis

LAND

SUPER-SMART COMBAT TANKS

62 How technology is making tanks super

TIGER I

38 Inside the Wehrmacht's fearsome WWII tank

20

"THE M551 SHERIDAN WAS CAPABLE OF AIR-DROPPING FROM A CARGO PLANE"

LIGHT TANKS

HUMVEE

ROLLS ROYCE

SU-76M

LIGHT TANKS

Light tanks first saw action in WWI and demonstrated their versatility throughout the 20th century, before arguably becoming obsolete

RENAULT FT

Founded: 1917
Country: France
Often cited as the world's first 'modern' tank, the Renault FT was a stalwart towards the end of the First World War, with over 3,000 of them produced during that time. Five or six could be made for the price of a larger tank, and they were built to swarm larger enemies and defeat them by sheer numbers.

T-26

Founded: 1931
Country: Soviet Union
The Soviet T-26 was heavily based on the Vickers Mark-E light tank operated by the British, and became an admirable model for rapid production. It's quite remarkable that over 10,000 of these machines were operational by 1939, cementing the Soviet Union's reputation as a military industrial powerhouse.

M3 STUART

Founded: 1940
Country: USA
The M3 is certainly one of the most well-known light tanks ever built, and was produced in large numbers by the US during the war. Many of these Stuarts would be leased to Commonwealth forces, and a large number of them saw action in North Africa against Rommel's fearsome Afrika Korps.

M551 SHERIDAN

Founded: 1966
Country: USA
Built to replace the heavy M41 Walker Bulldog, the Sheridan tank was used extensively during the Vietnam War as a reconnaissance and light infantry support vehicle. This was despite its weak hull armor and subsequent vulnerability when faced with RPG fire or AT mines.

TYPE 95 HA-GO

Founded: 1936
Country: Japan
Due to the demand for faster and more-reliable armor, the Japanese brought this light tank into production a few years before the outbreak of WWII. Its Hotchkiss-inspired cannon was built for dispensing with infantry, and two Type 97 LMGs completed the arsenal.

FV-101 SCORPION

Founded: 1972
Country: United Kingdom
Some Scorpions are believed to still be in use today around the world, with half of those produced being allocated for export. Only weighing eight tons, the Scorpion was an ideal vehicle for infantry support and reconnaissance, seeing action in the First Gulf War as well as the Falkland Islands conflict in 1982.

TYPE 62

Founded: 1962
Country: China
The Type 62 was built with maneuverability in mind, as well as economy. Due to its low cost it was adopted by certain African nations for use domestically, and the overall design was derived from the Soviet T-54. It first saw action in Vietnam after the Chinese provided several of the units to the NVA prior to the invasion of Kampuchea.

5 Facts about LIGHT TANKS

DROPPED ON PANAMA
The American M551 Sheridan was actually capable of being air-dropped from a cargo plane, with this being achieved for the first time during the US invasion of Panama.

EQUAL OPPORTUNITIES
The French Renault FT was available in both male and female varieties. The more common female carried a mounted machine gun, while the male sported a short-barreled 37mm gun.

THE MAE WEST TANK
During the Thirties, American troops nicknamed some of the early dual-turreted light tanks 'Mae West', as an homage to the decidedly busty movie star of the time.

A STRANGE EXPERIMENT
In 1942, the Soviet Union tested, somewhat successfully, a flying light tank. The A-40 was attached to a pair of wings that allowed it to be towed in mid air and then released onto the battlefield.

THE RECORD-BREAKER
The British Scorpion Peacekeeper tank was recognized by Guinness World Records as the fastest tank ever created, achieving an incredible 51mph on a test track in 2002.

Alamy; Corbis

LIGHT TANKS OF THE WORLD

Stretching track marks across the globe and throughout the 20th century

❶ SIEGE OF TOBRUK

TOBRUK, LIBYA 10 APRIL 1941

Large numbers of light tanks from the British Commonwealth go into fierce battles with Rommel's armored Afrika Korps to protect the Allied toehold in Eygpt.

Britain's General Bernard L Montgomery in North Africa

Vickers 6-ton

Landsverk L-120
Operating: 1937
Speciality: Defence and infantry support
Location: Sweden

Vickers 6-ton
Operating: 1929
Speciality: Long-range cross-country maneuvers
Location: United Kingdom

T15
Operating: 1936
Speciality: High-speed off-road maneuvers
Location: Belgium

Hotchkiss H35
Operating: 1935
Speciality: Engaging other light tanks
Location: France

Verdeja 1
Operating: 1940
Speciality: Infantry support and assault
Location: Spain

SK-105 Kürassier
Operating: 1967
Speciality: Anti-tank operations
Location: Austria

US LIGHT TANKS

M2 Light Tank
Operating: 1935
Speciality: Anti-infantry operations

M41 Walker Bulldog
Operating: 1953
Speciality: Scouting and infantry support

M22 Locust
Operating: 1942
Speciality: Airborne support and recon

TAM
Operating: 1976
Speciality: Infantry combat and wading
Location: Argentina

Argentine TAM

M22 Locust

❷ D-DAY

NORMANDY, FRANCE 6 JUNE 1944

The Normandy landings of Operation Overlord required the Allies to deposit a large amount of armor onto French shores. Among these were British and American light tanks, along with the near ubiquitous Sherman.

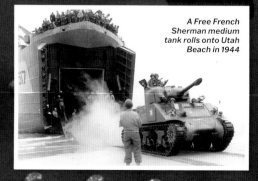
A Free French Sherman medium tank rolls onto Utah Beach in 1944

❸ FIRST BATTLE OF NAKTONG BULGE
SOUTH KOREA 6 AUGUST 1950

North Korea crosses the Naktong River and into US-held South Korean territory. The Americans are on stand-by with M24 Chaffee light tanks, which saw service until after Vietnam.

The Soviet offensive at Kursk put the Germans on the back foot

RUSSIAN LIGHT TANKS

PT-76
Operating: 1951
Speciality: Recon and troop support

T-18
Operating: 1928
Speciality: Strength and its firepower

Russian T-18

M1985
Operating: 1985
Speciality: Amphibious reconnaissance and assault
Location: North Korea

❺ BATTLE OF STALINGRAD
STALINGRAD, RUSSIA 2 FEBRUARY 1943

The German army surrenders at Stalingrad following a fierce counter-attack from the Soviet Union and its bevy of light tanks. Many cite this defeat as the turning point of the war on the Russian Front.

❻ BATTLE OF KURSK
KURSK, RUSSIA 5 JULY 1943

Georgiy Zhukov springs his armored trap on the Axis. American M3 tanks are utilized by the Soviet Union during some of the fiercest tank fighting ever known, although they prove unpopular.

French AMX-13

Type 63A
Operating: 1997
Speciality: Long-range amphibious assaults
Location: China

❼ THE BURMA FRONT
BURMA 20 FEBRUARY 1942

The 7th Armored Division, famously christened the Desert Rats, reaches Rangoon in Burma with light tanks and cruisers in order to set up defences in an attempt to halt the Japanese invasion of mainland Asia.

❽ SIX DAY WAR
SINAI PENINSULA, EGYPT 5 JUNE 1967

Israel and a conglomerate of Arab territories go toe to toe in the Six Day War, each utilizing a host of different light tank designs including AMX-13s and Soviet PT-76s.

Type 63A

❹ SECOND BATTLE OF EL ALAMEIN
EL ALAMEIN, EGYPT 23 OCTOBER 1942

German Panzer II tanks face off against a cohort of Crusader Mk I tanks of Great Britain as Monty goes head-to-head with Rommel.

British Crusader tanks move into position in North Africa

HEAD TO HEAD

War rages on the Eastern Front as the old Wehrmacht war horse, the Panzer I, goes up against the new kid on the block, the Soviet T-70

T-70

YEARS IN OPERATION: *1942-1948*
LOYALTY: *USSR* NUMBER MADE: *8,200*

FIREPOWER

Surprisingly heavy for a light tank, the T-70 had a 45mm gun that used both armor-piercing and explosive rounds. Its secondary weapon was a 7.622mm machine gun.

SPEED

The T-70 had 140 horsepower at its disposal, which gave it a top speed of 28mph. Light tanks had to be quick to compensate for their thin armor.

TACTICS

With a crew of two, the T-70 struggled to use its main turret effectively and became more of a reconnaissance vehicle. Its chassis would later be used for SU-76M tank killers and the T-80.

RANGE

A fuel capacity of 120 US Gallons gave the T-70 a range of 224 miles and helped it zoom across the Eastern Front, where it regularly supported the medium T-34 tank in battle.

ARMOR

Protection began at 35mm, but increased to 45mm in later models. The armor was reasonable, but wasn't enough to shield the T-70 from larger tanks and artillery on the battlefield.

LEGACY

It may have been the most produced Soviet light tank of the war but the T-70 quickly became obsolete and was quickly changed to an anti-tank vehicle to suit its qualities.

TOTAL

SOVIET TANK PRODUCTION

Churning out T-70s like there was no tomorrow, the Soviet production line was bolstered by the decision to turn civilian factories into military production centers. The T-70 itself was often partnered with the T-34 on the battlefield as they fought the Germans at huge battles such as Kursk. Before the end of the war it was effectively replaced by the T-80, and its chassis was used on tank destroyers like the SU-76M and anti-aircraft guns such as the ZSU-37 as battlefield tactics and technology began to veer away from lighter tanks towards heavier, stronger models.

While the Germans were focusing on quality, the Soviets went for sheer numbers. The tactic worked, as the Wehrmacht was overwhelmed

PANZER I

YEARS IN OPERATION: **1935-1945**
LOYALTY: **NAZI GERMANY** NUMBER MADE: **2,800**

FIREPOWER

The Panzer I lacked a main gun, instead employing two 7.92mm MG-13 machine guns that could fire 650 rounds per minute and had 2,250 rounds of ammunition.

SPEED

Being an older tank, the Panzer could only muster 25mph, but in the early days of the war that was more than enough to operate as an effective troop support.

TACTICS

The Panzer I was incredibly effective in the opening exchanges of the war as it stormed out of Germany as one of the main components of blitzkrieg.

RANGE

The Panzer could traverse 87 miles without filling up, which proved to be more than enough for the rapid assaults of 'lightning war'.

ARMOR

The steel-plated armor of a Panzer I was some of the most primitive in the German armored division, only a mere 12.5mm in thickness.

LEGACY

Even though light tanks were superseded by heavier models in the Wehrmacht, the Panzer I was the starting point for German tank production and showed their intent on rearmament.

TOTAL

The German tank production line was efficient, but could not match the output of the Allied powers

GERMAN TANK PRODUCTION

Throughout World War I, Germany had seemingly very little interest in tanks, but this changed dramatically in the vast rearmament of the Thirties. The first tank to appear on the Wehrmacht production line and breach the Versailles treaty was the Panzerkampfwagen I. The model was used extensively on both the Western and Eastern Fronts and became a major element of blitzkrieg. As time wore on, the Third Reich changed its focus from light tanks to medium and heavy Panzers such as the Tiger and Panther, but the legacy of the Panzer I lived on.

"THE PANZER I WAS INCREDIBLY EFFECTIVE IN THE OPENING EXCHANGES OF THE WAR AS IT STORMED OUT OF GERMANY AS ONE OF THE MAIN COMPONENTS OF BLITZKRIEG"

ANATOMY OF A...
PANZER II

Developed clandestinely before the invasion of Poland, the Panzer II was phased out from 1942, though its chassis was used on a number of self-propelled guns until 1944

7.92MM COAXIAL MASCHINENGEWEHR
Also known by the designation MG 34, the 7.92 machine gun fitted to the Panzer II was an effective anti-infantry weapon and also saw service as a support weapon among Wehrmacht platoons

HATCH FOR ENTRY OR ESCAPE

20MM MAIN GUN
Produced in Germany in the mid-to-late Thirties, the 2cm KwK 30 L/55 was based on a 20mm flak cannon and was fully automatic, requiring the operator to fire in controlled bursts

THE TRACKS

THE FRONTAL GLACIS
These only sported the standard amount of armor, which was strange for a tank, but later received a new single piece 30mm glacis upon reaching its final Ausf F designation

PANZERKAMPFWAGEN II

YEARS IN USE: 9
COUNTRY OF ORIGIN: GERMANY
ENGINE SIZE: 6-CYLINDER, 138HP
CREW: 3
LENGTH: 4.81M
WEIGHT: 8.9 TONS
TOP SPEED: 25MPH
WEAPONS: 1 X 20MM KWK 30 MAIN GUN,
1 X 7.92MM COAXIAL MACHINE GUN

MANUAL TRANSMISSION SYSTEM
The Panzer II sported a six-speed plus reverse manual gearbox made by ZF Friedrichshafen, which was generally considered to be reliable. Reversing was particularly handy for these little tanks

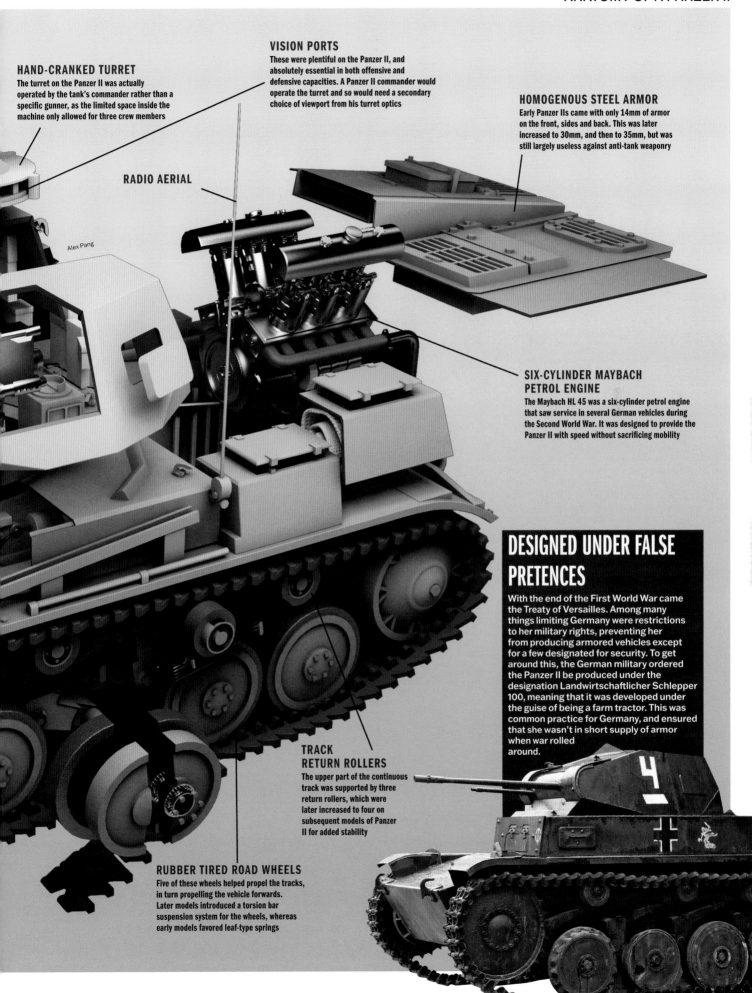

HAND-CRANKED TURRET
The turret on the Panzer II was actually operated by the tank's commander rather than a specific gunner, as the limited space inside the machine only allowed for three crew members

VISION PORTS
These were plentiful on the Panzer II, and absolutely essential in both offensive and defensive capacities. A Panzer II commander would operate the turret and so would need a secondary choice of viewport from his turret optics

HOMOGENOUS STEEL ARMOR
Early Panzer IIs came with only 14mm of armor on the front, sides and back. This was later increased to 30mm, and then to 35mm, but was still largely useless against anti-tank weaponry

RADIO AERIAL

Alex Pang

SIX-CYLINDER MAYBACH PETROL ENGINE
The Maybach HL 45 was a six-cylinder petrol engine that saw service in several German vehicles during the Second World War. It was designed to provide the Panzer II with speed without sacrificing mobility

DESIGNED UNDER FALSE PRETENCES

With the end of the First World War came the Treaty of Versailles. Among many things limiting Germany were restrictions to her military rights, preventing her from producing armored vehicles except for a few designated for security. To get around this, the German military ordered the Panzer II be produced under the designation Landwirtschaftlicher Schlepper 100, meaning that it was developed under the guise of being a farm tractor. This was common practice for Germany, and ensured that she wasn't in short supply of armor when war rolled around.

TRACK RETURN ROLLERS
The upper part of the continuous track was supported by three return rollers, which were later increased to four on subsequent models of Panzer II for added stability

RUBBER TIRED ROAD WHEELS
Five of these wheels helped propel the tracks, in turn propelling the vehicle forwards. Later models introduced a torsion bar suspension system for the wheels, whereas early models favored leaf-type springs

ROLLS-ROYCE

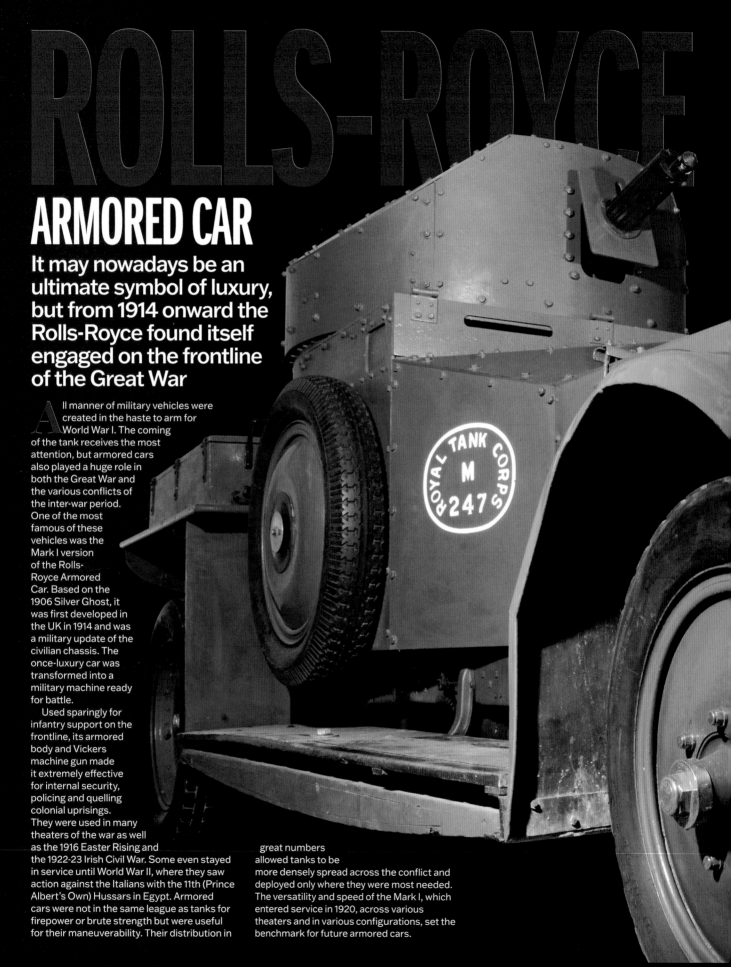

ARMORED CAR

It may nowadays be an ultimate symbol of luxury, but from 1914 onward the Rolls-Royce found itself engaged on the frontline of the Great War

All manner of military vehicles were created in the haste to arm for World War I. The coming of the tank receives the most attention, but armored cars also played a huge role in both the Great War and the various conflicts of the inter-war period. One of the most famous of these vehicles was the Mark I version of the Rolls-Royce Armored Car. Based on the 1906 Silver Ghost, it was first developed in the UK in 1914 and was a military update of the civilian chassis. The once-luxury car was transformed into a military machine ready for battle.

Used sparingly for infantry support on the frontline, its armored body and Vickers machine gun made it extremely effective for internal security, policing and quelling colonial uprisings. They were used in many theaters of the war as well as the 1916 Easter Rising and the 1922-23 Irish Civil War. Some even stayed in service until World War II, where they saw action against the Italians with the 11th (Prince Albert's Own) Hussars in Egypt. Armored cars were not in the same league as tanks for firepower or brute strength but were useful for their maneuverability. Their distribution in great numbers allowed tanks to be more densely spread across the conflict and deployed only where they were most needed. The versatility and speed of the Mark I, which entered service in 1920, across various theaters and in various configurations, set the benchmark for future armored cars.

The Irish purchased armored cars in large quantities after the 1922-23 civil war

ROLLS-ROYCE ARMORED CAR MARK I

MANUFACTURED: 1920
ORIGIN: UK
LENGTH: 16.4 FEET
WEIGHT: 4.7 TONS
ENGINE: SIX CYLINDER
FUEL: PETROL

MAXIMUM SPEED: 60MPH
CREW: 3-4
PRIMARY WEAPON: .303 WATER-COOLED VICKERS MACHINE GUN
SECONDARY WEAPONS: HOTCHKISS AIR-COOLED MACHINE GUN, CREW'S SIDEARMS

"ITS ARMORED BODY AND VICKERS MACHINE GUN MADE IT EXTREMELY EFFECTIVE FOR INTERNAL SECURITY, POLICING AND QUELLING COLONIAL UPRISINGS"

This is the 1920 Pattern (E1949.329) version of the Rolls-Royce

The Vickers was used on a ball-mounting mechanism, which improved its aim and range of fire

VICKERS MACHINE GUN

The main armament of the Rolls-Royce Armored Car was a .303 water-cooled Vickers machine gun. Operating from the self-turning turret above, the gunner could spray their target with bullets while being shielded from return fire. The Vickers was used extensively in all theaters of World War I and was an effective weapon against infantry. On the armored car, it could suppress insurgents and uprisings with ease. As well as the Vickers, each member of the crew carried sidearms, and a Hotchkiss air-cooled machine gun was often stowed aboard for dismounted use.

The engine had some of the thickest armor plating on the whole vehicle as the car would be a sitting duck if it were disabled

Although the tires were vulnerable to gunfire, there are few reports of them being punctured

"OPERATING FROM THE SELF-TURNING TURRET ABOVE, THE GUNNER COULD SPRAY THEIR TARGET WITH BULLETS WHILE BEING SHIELDED FROM FIRE"

A crank handle was used to start up the engine, which was not ideal for conflict situations

WHEELS AND TIRES

The metallic rims of the car's four wheels allowed it to traverse boggy ground and dirt tracks as well as tarmac and paved roads. The wheels were not protected by armor and punctures from gunfire could be an issue with the Mark I, so two spare tires on either side were provided. The rear wheels were twin disc while the front two were single disc. As time wore on and newer updates arrived, the wheels were made thicker to protect them from punctures and improve the ride quality.

ROLLS-ROYCE ENGINE

The heavy armored body of the Rolls-Royce peaked at 13mm thick in critical spots, so a powerful engine was required to shift the bulk. A six-cylinder water-cooled engine ran with minimal vibration and noise, which helped enormously with the armored car's reconnaissance capabilities. The Mark I may have weighed 10,337 pounds but the engine still gave the vehicle 80 horsepower (60 kilowatts), which allowed it to reach a top speed of 60mph. The engine itself was covered in armor to protect it from gunfire.

ARMORED CARS THROUGH THE 20TH CENTURY
HOW THESE MACHINES DEVELOPED FROM THE ROLLS-ROYCE TEMPLATE

SCHWERER PANZERSPÄHWAGEN

A loophole in the Treaty of Versailles meant there was no limit on German armored car production. The Wehrmacht generals used this to their advantage and soon produced a fleet of Schwerer Panzerspähwagen (heavy reconnaissance armored cars). During the war, they were primarily used as scout vehicles and came in six and eight-wheel versions.

BA-64

Coming into service in 1942, more than 9,000 of these lightly armored vehicles were produced by the USSR. Skipping across the battlefields, it was used to quickly and safely transport army officers. Its speed and mobility made it a useful asset on the Eastern Front against the armies of the Third Reich.

M1117 ARMORED SECURITY VEHICLE

Used frequently by the US Army from its inception in 1999, the M1117 is the modern update of the armored car. Essentially a heavy-duty version of the popular Humvee, it has been used extensively in conflicts in the Middle East and was developed after the Battle of Mogadishu.

The rear side of the Rolls-Royce was an open tray and was very different to the pre-war civilian version

The driver saw the road ahead through a narrow opening that helped protect the occupants from gunfire and shrapnel

The riveted steel armor protected the engine and was continually reinforced and strengthened in later models of the armored car

SV 4996

REAR DECK

With only limited space for the crew of four inside the turret, the rear deck of the vehicle was utilized to carry extra loads. The crew's food and water was located here as well as other supplies and tools for maintenance in case of breakdown. Extra weapons and ammunition were also kept here for longer conflicts. The design made the Mark I look like a pickup truck and the Hotchkiss machine gun could be set up on the rear to fire from the back of the vehicle.

Extra support troops could hop on for a ride on the small bench on the back of the vehicle

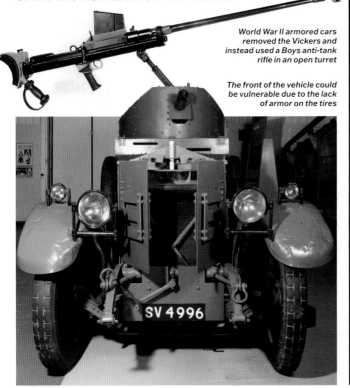

The car's side panels provided extra space to carry soldiers and supplies

"ARMORED CARS WERE ALSO USED EXTENSIVELY IN LAWRENCE OF ARABIA'S OPERATIONS AGAINST THE TURKS"

World War II armored cars removed the Vickers and instead used a Boys anti-tank rifle in an open turret

The front of the vehicle could be vulnerable due to the lack of armor on the tires

SV 4996

ARMORED CARS ACROSS THE EMPIRE
THE ROLLS-ROYCE WAS SENT OUT ACROSS THE WORLD TO ASSIST THE BRITISH WAR EFFORT

WORLD WAR I

At the start of the war, armored cars were quickly snapped up by the RNAS (Royal Naval Air Service) for use on patrols in Dunkirk. They were also used extensively in Lawrence of Arabia's operations against the Turks. Two squadrons were even sent to Gallipoli, one of Britain's biggest failures of the war.

IRISH CIVIL WAR

After being used to help quash the 1916 Easter Rising, the Rolls-Royce was once again pressed into action across the Irish Sea in the 1922-23 civil war. Fighting on the side of the Irish Free State Government, they participated in street conflicts in Dublin, Cork and Waterford.

WORLD WAR II

Despite being relatively dated, there were still 76 Mark I 1924 Pattern vehicles in active service in 1941. An upgrade of the original model had also been commissioned and was called the Fordson. Equipped with a Boys anti-tank rifle, it policed the British-occupied Middle East.

THE TANK MUSEUM

Situated in the Bovington Army Camp in Dorset, The Tank Museum was opened in 1947. It contains more than 300 vehicles from 26 different countries, from the World War I Mark I tank to the currently serving Challenger 2. The Rolls-Royce Armored Car was given to the museum in 1949 and is still in good working order. The Rolls-Royce opens the show at the museum's yearly Tankfest event, the world's best display of historic moving armor, held on the last weekend of June.

Visit www.tankmuseum.org for the museum's opening hours and admission information.

Images: Bovington Tank Museum

A7V TANK

One of the earliest tanks to be produced, the A7V was supposed to deliver German soldiers a mobile fortress to break through Allied lines, but it wasn't a great success

Designed specifically to counter the emergence of British tanks on the Western Front during World War I, the A7V was a medium-armored tank designed by the German General War Department in 1916. The vehicle resembled a mobile pillbox or armored personnel carrier and delivered a steel-plated body with the capacity to hold 18 soldiers, a 2.2-inch cannon and six to eight 0.3-inch machine guns. For a full hardware breakdown, see the diagram to the right. Its role, as hinted at by its German classification – Sturmpanzer-Kraftwagen – translates roughly as 'assault armored motor vehicle' – was to assault and break through fortified Allied lines, as armies became increasingly entrenched.

The first pre-production A7V was delivered in September 1917 and was closely followed by the first production model in October of the same year. Despite this, the first deployment of the A7V had to wait until March 1918, when five of the 20 made were deployed north of the Saint Quentin Canal in northern France. Unfortunately, this is where the first design flaws of the vehicle were initially encountered. Three of the five

tanks broke down during operation due to mechanical faults. Despite these issues, the A7V fleet was then deployed en masse, with 18 vehicles participating in the Second Battle of Villers-Bretonneux in April 1918.

Although reports from Allied soldiers at the time state that the A7V's armor made direct attack from their handheld weapons impossible, the A7V's modest armor was easily breached by the Allied Mark IV's six-pounder cannons. Furthermore, due to the low clearance and crude design of the A7V's suspension and tracks, many got stuck on difficult off-road terrain and two even toppled into holes. In addition, after a swift counterattack by Allied forces, three of the stranded A7Vs were captured.

As such, even though 100 A7Vs had originally been ordered, their limited impact led to the program being scrapped, with many of the remaining vehicles dismantled as early as October 1918. Today, no original A7V has survived, with the majority scrapped. However, a replica based on original designs was built between 1987 and 1990 and can now be viewed at the Panzermuseum in Munster, Germany.

A replica of an A7V based on original schematics is viewable today at the Panzermuseum in Munster, Germany

ANATOMY OF AN A7V

WE BREAK DOWN THIS WORLD WAR I TANK TO SEE HOW IT WAS BUILT AND HOW IT OPERATED

ARMOR

Despite having 20mm (1.2in) steel plate at the sides, 30mm (0.8in) at the front and 10mm (0.4in) on the roof, the A7V was easily penetrated by cannon fire. This was because the steel was not hardened armor plate. As such, it could only stop small arms fire

ARMAMENT

The main weapon of the A7V was a 57mm (2.2in) Maxim-Nordenfelt cannon, which was equipped to all male variants. The secondary armament was a series of six to eight 7.9mm (0.3in) MG08 machine guns. The tank could also carry 180 shells for the cannon

CREW

An A7V's crew consisted of 17 soldiers and one officer. These were needed for the following roles: commander, driver, mechanic, two artillery men (gunner and loader) and 12 infantry men (six gunners and six loaders)

A shot of an A7V and its crew from July 1918

Despite the A7V being capable of traveling at 9mph, it frequently got stuck on uneven ground

"MANY GOT STUCK ON DIFFICULT OFF-ROAD TERRAIN AND TWO EVEN TOPPLED INTO HOLES"

A7V

CREW 18
HEIGHT 11FT
WIDTH 10FT
LENGTH 24FT
WEIGHT 30 TONS
ENGINE 2 X DAIMLER FOUR-CYLINDER PETROL (149KW/200HP TOTAL)
SUSPENSION HOLT TRACK, VERTICAL SPRINGS
MAX SPEED 9MPH
MAX RANGE 50MI
ARMOR SIDES: 0.8IN; FRONT: 1.2IN; ROOF: 0.4IN
MAIN ARMAMENT 2.2IN MAXIM-NORDENFELT CANNON
SECONDARY ARMAMENT 6 X 0.3IN MG08 GUNS

ENGINE

The A7V's power came courtesy of two centrally mounted Daimler four-cylinder petrol engines, each capable of generating 75kW (100hp). The engines were fed by a 500l (132ga) fuel tank. At full power, the A7V could travel at a maximum speed of 9mph

SUSPENSION

The A7V was equipped with helical springs, rear-drive sprockets, front-mounted idlers and 24 roller wheels in bogies. The lack of shock absorbers made the ride incredibly bumpy and the low clearance (ie 190-400mm/7.5-15.7in) led to poor off-road capabilities

An A7V on the Western Front in March 1918

TIGER I

One of the most advanced Axis panzers of the Second World War, the Tiger I struck fear into the hearts of Allied tank divisions

Between August 1942 and the fall of the Third Reich, approximately 1,500 Panzerkampfwagen VI Tiger Ausf.E were manufactured by the Nazi war machine.

Renowned for its accuracy and strong armor, this heavy tank was a formidable foe to the Allied forces. It outclassed many of the Sherman tank models in several departments and tales told from the war have described 75mm rounds bouncing straight off the Tiger's solid armor.

The tank saw its first action in September 1942 as the Third Reich advanced eastwards under Operation Barbarossa. In an engagement near Leningrad, four Tigers managed to dispatch 24 Soviet T-34 tanks. In fact, the Tiger only floundered when it ended up becoming stuck in the harsh conditions of the

PANZERKAMPFWAGEN VI TIGER AUSF.E

COMMISSIONED: AUGUST 1942
ORIGIN: KASSEL, GERMANY
LENGTH: 27.7FT
RANGE: 16,404FT
ARMOR: ELECTRO-WELDED INTERLOCKING NICKEL-STEEL PLATES
ENGINE: MAYBACH HL 210 P45
PRIMARY WEAPON: 88MM CANNON
SECONDARY WEAPONS: 7.92MM MG-34 MACHINE GUNS
CREW: 5

Russian winter, where its caterpillar tracks would be repeatedly trapped in the dense, frozen mud of Eastern Europe. This meant the nimble T-34 could now outmaneuver the Tiger and strike where the armor was weakest. The Allies had no answer to the sheer power of Panzerkampfwagen VIs until the development of the Sherman Firefly in 1943, which finally matched Tigers pound-for-pound. Before this, only wave after wave of Shermans and T-34s could bring about the downfall of a Tiger.

By 1944, German factories had hurried the Tiger II into production and the numbers of the Tiger I dwindled. Contemporary reports suggest that the Tiger I was over-engineered and, towards the latter stages of its lifespan, rushed off the production line as the Nazis desperately tried to save the war.

A Tiger I tank rolling across the battlefields of Europe was a frightening sight for any Allied soldier

"THE ALLIES HAD NO ANSWER TO THE SHEER POWER OF PANZERKAMPFWAGEN VIs UNTIL THE DEVELOPMENT OF THE SHERMAN FIREFLY"

131

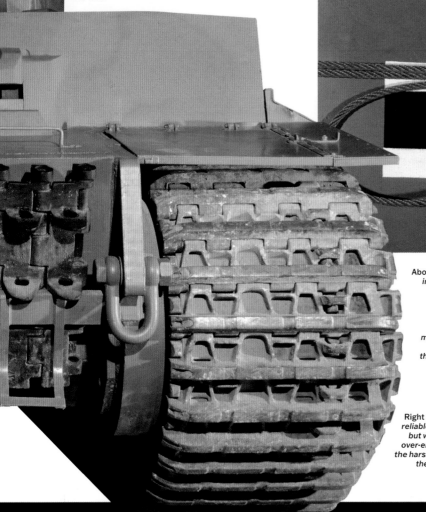

Above *The tank has insignia showing its battalion and allegiance to the German Wehrmacht. This particular model was found abandoned in the North African desert*

Right *The Tiger I was reliable mechanically but was let down by over-engineering and the harsh conditions of the Eastern Front*

88MM GUN

The main weapon of the Tiger could shatter the defences of Allied tanks and fortifications. The 88mm gun could penetrate 100mm of armor from up to 3,280 feet away. On the battlefield, the Tiger would be strategically placed on hilltops to make use of its cannon's long range while being protected from enemy fire by its thick armor.

Above: The panzer's ammunition varied from armor-piercing shots to high explosive and incendiary rounds

The huge 88mm Panzergranate 39 gun dwarfed the allied M4 Sherman cannon and was originally an anti-aircraft gun

CATERPILLAR TRACKS

The tracks fitted on a Tiger were extremely wide. This helped the bulky 57-ton tank traverse over boggy ground as well as spreading the weight more thinly to cross bridges. Despite this, the Tiger was the victim of adverse weather conditions on the Eastern Front as frozen mud wedged itself within the tracks. The lightweight soviet T-34s didn't experience this problem as frequently and were able to outflank the Nazi tanks – particularly at the 1943 Battle of Kursk, which was the biggest tank battle of all time.

SECONDARY WEAPONS AND AMMUNITION (TWO 7.92 MG-34 MACHINE GUNS)

As well as its main cannon, the Tiger was fitted with MG-34 or MG-42 machine guns. A Tiger tank would have one next to the driver at the front of the tank and on some models an MG would be attached to the top of the vehicle. These machine guns could reach distances of up to 1,312ft and 5,850 rounds would be kept aboard to cut down swathes of infantry and light vehicles.

THE TIGER II
THE TIGER WASN'T THE MOST FEARSOME OF THE NAZI PANZERS. THE TIGER II WAS BIGGER, STRONGER AND BETTER PROTECTED

MAIN GUN
The Tiger II's main gun packed a marginally more powerful punch than the Tiger I as it could penetrate 182mm (seven inches) of armor at double the distance. This was also further than Allied tanks of the period. Known informally as the Königstiger, only 492 of these mighty machines were made.

ARMOR
The armor was nearly 200mm thick on the Tiger II, and significantly thicker than its predecessor. The Allies tried to create equivalents, but tanks like the American T29 were not ready for World War Two. The Tiger IIs were rushed into production and were often hampered by ill-suited engines.

KING-SIZE
The Tiger II was a heavy tank and its bulk was even larger than the Tiger I. The original Tiger already had issues with its engine so the larger size of the Tiger II emphasized these problems even more. Only in use at the tail-end of the war, we will never know how it could have contributed to the earlier stages of the conflict.

Images: Bundesarchiv, Hamann / Wagner

INTERIOR

The Tiger's small enclosed interior contained a crew of five: a gunner, loader, driver, commander and a radio operator. Although small, the Tigers were over-engineered by their manufacturers, so the interior was packed with modern sighting equipment, weapons caches and tools. The drivetrain was aided by hydraulic-power-assisted steering and the entire mechanism was powered by four batteries. The whole tank was so advanced that when it was captured by the British, it was inspected by Winston Churchill and George VI and then taken back to Britain for extensive testing.

Despite its large exterior, the inside of a Tiger was a cramped place where fires were a frequent problem

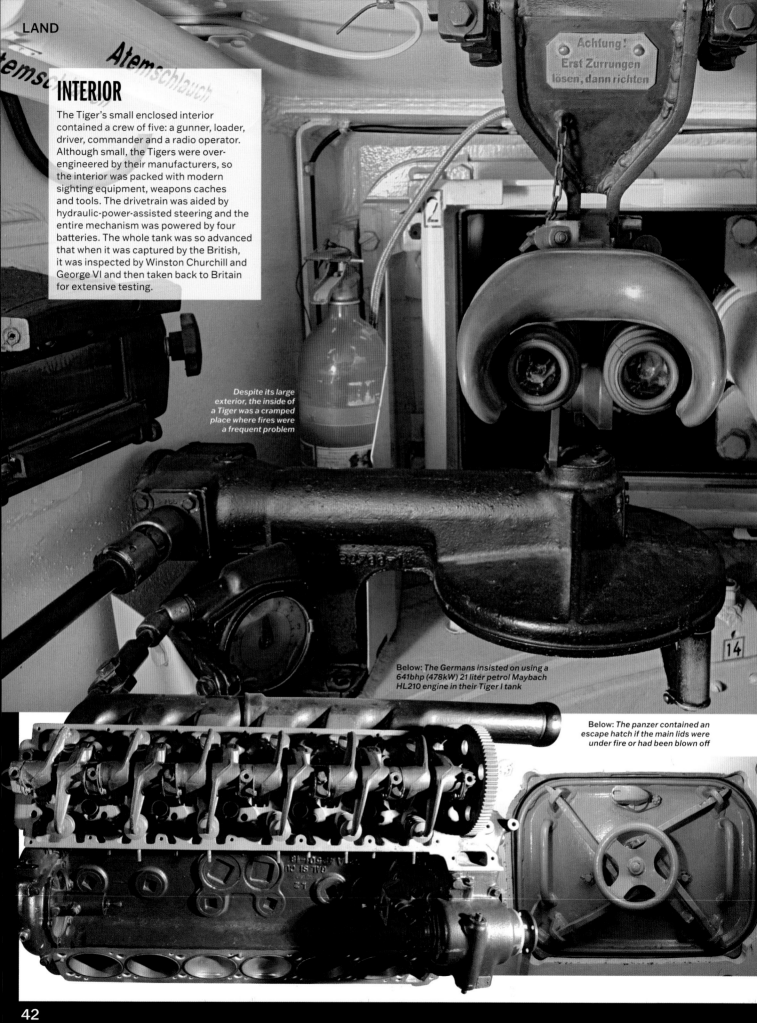

Below: *The Germans insisted on using a 641bhp (478kW) 21 liter petrol Maybach HL210 engine in their Tiger I tank*

Below: *The panzer contained an escape hatch if the main lids were under fire or had been blown off*

As well as the 88mm and the MG32 machine gun(s), the Tiger also had two sets of three smokescreen canisters to conceal its panzer and cause confusion

THE TIGER 131

This Tiger model was part of the 504 Schwere Panzer Battalion in North Africa and was one of the very few not to have been destroyed by its own crew. Forensics and analysis have shown that the Tiger was hit several times by British Churchill tanks but none disabled the tank. The main damage was dealt just underneath the barrel and wedged the turret to the hull. This stopped it from working, but could easily have been repaired by the crew. This makes it even stranger that the crew abandoned it and didn't destroy it as they were instructed to. It's the only working Tiger currently in existence and was featured in the 2014 film Fury.

Below: The well-engineered Tiger was a box of tricks and had cables and even a spade to help retrieve it from sticky situations

The Tiger had a complex exhaust system on its rear to increase power

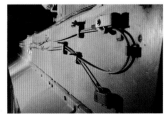

TIGERS? WHAT ABOUT PANTHERS?

Just below the heavy Tiger tank in the power stakes was the medium Panzer V or Panther tank. An excellent all-rounder, it had top of the range capabilities in everything from speed to firepower and maneuverability. The idea for the Panther came after the previous model of Panzer IV tanks were outclassed on the Eastern Front by the Soviet T-34. The Wehrmacht captured the Red Army's prize tank and got to work creating a better alternative. The Panther was born as a result. One of the Panther's first conflicts was at Kursk. Plagued by mechanical issues, it did not perform well in its first acid test, as the Wehrmacht lost out to the Red Army in what was the largest tank battle of all time. After this initial setback however, the Panzer V went from strength to strength and accounted for almost half of the German tanks on both the Western and Eastern fronts. Like the Tiger, it consistently outclassed both the M4 Sherman and the original T-34 but ultimately fell foul of the overwhelmingly superior Allied numbers, as well as the development of large guns to help effectively combat them.

The massive 88mm gun could take out almost everything on the Second World War battlefield

Above: *According to many historians, the Panther was the best tank of the entire Second World War*

THE THIRD REICH PRODUCTION LINE

The technology inside German tanks during the Second World War was second to none. However when the USA entered the war and the Soviet production line thudded into gear, the Third Reich simply could not cope. When Albert Speer became Minister of Armaments and War Production in 1942, the amount of panzers leaving the factories did increase but it was simply not enough. The issue was the German tendency to over-engineer their tanks. Despite boasting far better attributes than their rivals in almost every department, there simply weren't enough German tanks to hold the line on the battlefield. When the time of the Tiger I came about it was already too late, so they were mostly used, albeit very effectively, in a defensive capacity. On the Western Front in particular, the Tiger dominated the US M4 Sherman but as the Allied numbers poured through Europe and outflanked the Axis in Operation Overlord, even the powerful Tiger couldn't hold its ground. In the final year of the war, the German tanks were rushed through production so they could try and stem the flow of Allied troops. However this still posed problems as the engineering worsened and the German panzers, especially the Tiger II, suffered, and with failing Armored Divisions, the war was as good as lost.

The main lid was the primary entry to the tank and where the commander would look out to navigate and plan the route ahead

SHERMAN TANK

How this famous tank led the Allied war machines in WWII

The first use of the tank as a military weapon was in the First World War at the Battle of the Somme. Armored vehicles would become a big part of warfare, but it wasn't until the Second World War that they became essential. The most essential of all the Allied tanks was the Sherman.

Titled the M4 Medium Tank, it was named after William Tecumseh Sherman, who was a Union general in the American Civil War. It replaced the M3 armored vehicle and was provided as part of the American Lend-Lease policy to its allies. It was first used in 1942 by the British, to tussle with the German Panzer IIIs and IVs for battlefield supremacy.

The Sherman was based on speed and maneuverability. It had weaker armor and less equipment than its German counterparts and with the introduction of the Axis' Tiger and Panther models, it became inferior on the battlefield. This was soon remedied with the introduction of the Firefly, Jumbo and Easy Eight variants. The tank's main tactic was to fire an armor-piercing round and then incinerate the unarmored and exposed enemy tank. Shermans were always fielded in great numbers and worked well in partnership with M10 Tank Destroyers. The Sherman was used extensively in the African, French and Italian campaigns until the end of the war. Some models could attach a flamethrower, rocket launcher or bulldozer blade, as well as amphibious versions, which were used in the D-Day landings.

Even after the war had ended, the Sherman was still used frequently. Its reliability and low running cost allowed it to be deployed in the Korean War, as well as by other nations, with Australia, Brazil, Egypt and many more having their own specific variations of the successful Sherman model.

M4 SHERMAN

FIRST YEAR OF SERVICE 1942
AMOUNT MADE 50,000
CREW 5
LENGTH 19.16FT
WIDTH 8.6FT
HEIGHT 8.99FT
ENGINE 425HP
MAX RANGE 120MI
MAX SPEED 30MPH
WEAPONS 75MM MAIN GUM, 3X MACHINE GUNS

WHAT'S INSIDE?

DELVING UNDERNEATH THE BODYWORK OF A SHERMAN TANK

ENGINE
The engine was situated at the rear of the tank and varied between each model. They were made primarily by three US companies, General Motors, Ford and Chrysler

TURRET
The Sherman had a fully 360-degree traversing turret, which revolved on a rail using an electric system. Some versions, like the Sherman Badger, were turretless

TRACKS
Using a Vertical Volute Spring Suspension (VVSS), the tank had 78-link tracks, which was designed to put minimal pressure on the ground to keep it light and nimble on all terrain

LIBERTY

> "IT WAS NAMED AFTER WILLIAM TECUMSEH SHERMAN, WHO WAS A UNION GENERAL IN THE AMERICAL CIVIL WAR"

THE VARIOUS MEMBERS OF THE SHERMAN TANK FAMILY

1 M4A3E2 Jumbo
Designed for the liberation of Europe, the Jumbo weighed 38 tons. It was very well protected, resisting all German anti-tank guns.

2 M4A3E8 Easy Eight
Smaller and more mobile yet with the same armor as the Jumbo, this variant saw frequent postwar service, including in Vietnam.

3 M4A3R3 Zippo
Known as a 'flamethrower tank', designed to flush out pillboxes and bunkers, it was mainly used in the Far East theater of war.

4 T34 Calliope
Carrying a rocket launcher, this tank variation only came into use at the tail-end of WWII but was highly effective against fortified defences.

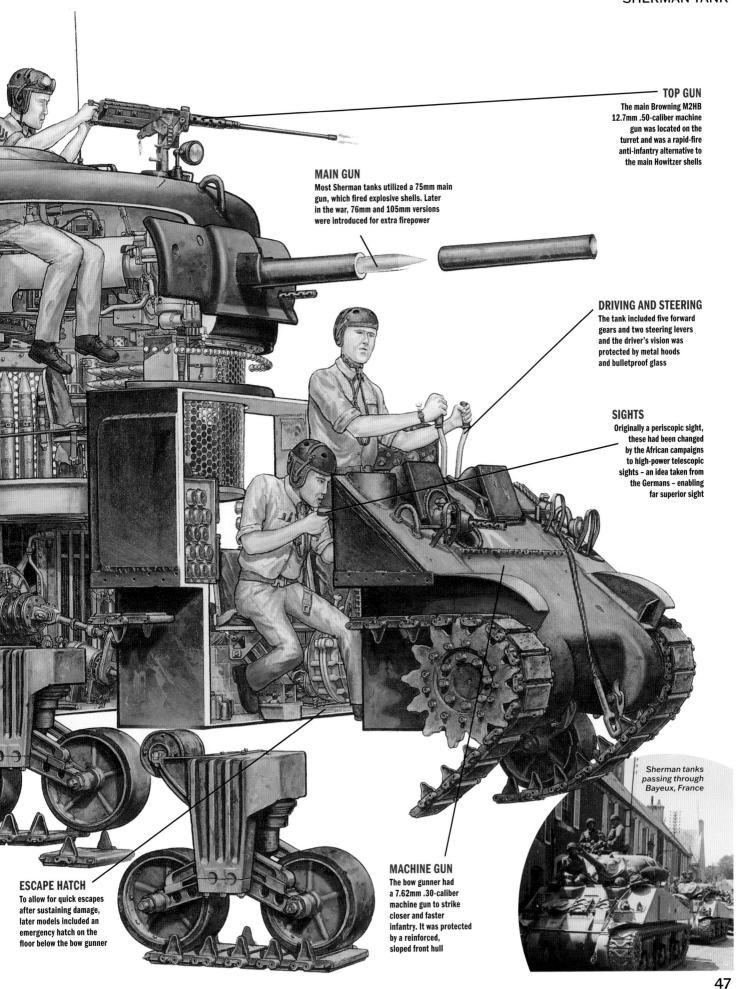

TOP GUN
The main Browning M2HB 12.7mm .50-caliber machine gun was located on the turret and was a rapid-fire anti-infantry alternative to the main Howitzer shells

MAIN GUN
Most Sherman tanks utilized a 75mm main gun, which fired explosive shells. Later in the war, 76mm and 105mm versions were introduced for extra firepower

DRIVING AND STEERING
The tank included five forward gears and two steering levers and the driver's vision was protected by metal hoods and bulletproof glass

SIGHTS
Originally a periscopic sight, these had been changed by the African campaigns to high-power telescopic sights – an idea taken from the Germans – enabling far superior sight

Sherman tanks passing through Bayeux, France

MACHINE GUN
The bow gunner had a 7.62mm .30-caliber machine gun to strike closer and faster infantry. It was protected by a reinforced, sloped front hull

ESCAPE HATCH
To allow for quick escapes after sustaining damage, later models included an emergency hatch on the floor below the bow gunner

The Churchill tank typically operated with a five-man crew

The Churchill Mark IV weighed an incredible 38.5 tons

CHURCHILL TANK

The most successful British tank series during World War II, the Churchill was a defensive powerhouse and a versatile weapons platform

Designed in the aftermath of the evacuation of Dunkirk by the British Expeditionary Force, the Churchill tank was Britain's attempt to redress the technology gap between their aging Matilda II battalion and the German Panzer tanks that had them out-gunned. The result was the Mark I, a heavily armored battle tank equipped with a two-pounder main gun, three-inch howitzer in the rear and the most advanced and robust suspension system yet conceived. It was a defensive juggernaut, designed with one goal: to dominate the European theater of war.

From its introduction in June 1941, the tank proved a reliable and versatile weapon platform capable of engaging targets quickly and efficiently. Key to this was its high speed of 16mph and excellent turning ability, characteristics made possible by its multiple-bogie suspension system. The suspension was fitted to the hull under two large pannier enclosures on either side, with the tracks running over the top.

The tracks moved over a series of ten-inch wheels, which themselves were fitted to 11 bogies (a wheeled framework) on either side of the vehicle. The suspension took the main weight of the Churchill tank on nine of its 11 bogie pairs, with the front set used when nosing into the ground on steep terrain and the rear set used as a track tensioner. Due to the sheer number of wheels and wrap-round-pannier tracks, this allowed the Churchill tank to operate even when parts of the system

were damaged in combat, keeping the tank moving and operational.

Due to the weight of the Churchill's armor plating, a massive powerplant was necessary to keep it moving at speed. This power came courtesy of a Bedford Vehicles horizontally opposed twin-six petrol engine, which could produce 350bhp at 2,200rpm and delivered 960 pounds of torque. The engine was controlled through a Merritt-Brown gearbox with an in-built regenerative breaking system. This allowed the tank to be steered by changing the relative speeds of the two tracks and, when put in its lowest gear, perform a neutral turn on the spot. This ability to turn so rapidly earned the Churchill much praise and made engaging moving targets considerably easier than in previous models.

Initially, the Churchill was fitted with a two-pounder main gun and three-inch howitzer (artillery piece); however, the former was soon upgraded to a six-pounder cannon and the latter replaced with a high-caliber machine gun. These cannons gave the Churchill decent stopping power against medium armor, yet still left them short in firepower compared with their German counterparts. The Churchill's main cannon continued to be improved, with 75mm guns fitted to Mk IIIs.

Despite its average firepower, however, the Churchill's high maneuverability and excellent armor made it one of the foremost tanks of WWII, being extensively deployed in Europe and North Africa.

ARMAMENT
The Mk VII was armed with a 75mm cannon, which was housed in a composite turret. The gun allowed the tank to engage German armored vehicles and buildings, but lacked penetration against heavily armored targets. Machine guns and even flamethrowers were attached to other models

CREW
The Churchill was operated by five crew, consisting of a commander, gunner, radio operator, driver and co-driver. These inhabited four separate compartments within the hull, with the driving position located at the front, fighting compartment in the center and engine and gearbox areas in the rear

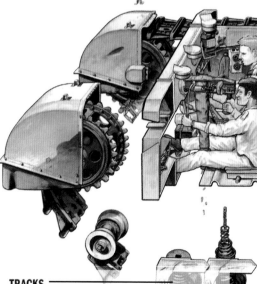

TRACKS
The Churchill was fitted with an advanced suspension system based on 11 bogies on either side, each carrying two ten-inch wheels. The vehicle's weight was taken by nine of the pairs at any one time, with the front pair used when nosing into the ground and the rear pair as a track tensioner

BLOWING THE LID OFF THE CHURCHILL MK VII

WE BREACH ONE OF THE MOST SUCCESSFUL CHURCHILL VARIANTS TO DISCOVER WHAT MADE IT SO RUTHLESS, RELIABLE AND ICONIC

A surviving Churchill mounted on top of a Churchill Bridgelayer's disconnected bridge

A Churchill Crocodile (converted Mk VII) featured a high-powered flamethrower capable of firing bursts over 150 yards

ARMOR
The Mk VII was nicknamed the 'Heavy Churchill' for its exceptional weight and protective armor. Its hull was 5.5in thick at the front, 2.2in thick at the sides and 2in thick at the rear. The turret was 5.9in thick at the front

CHURCHILL MK IV

CREW 5
WEIGHT 38.5 TONS
LENGTH 24FT 5IN
WIDTH 10FT 8IN
HEIGHT 8FT 2IN
ENGINE BEDFORD TWIN-SIX PETROL (350BHP AT 2,200RPM)
POWER/WEIGHT 9.1HP/TONNE
MAX RANGE 55MI
MAX SPEED 15MPH

MAXIMUM VERSATILITY

FROM BRIDGE LAYER TO MINE CLEARER, THE CHURCHILL TANK WAS THE IDEAL BASE FOR A HOST OF SPECIALIST VEHICLES

Due to the Churchill's high maneuverability and advanced suspension system, it made a natural base for a number of specialist vehicles. Some highlights include the Churchill Crocodile, a variant of the tank that was fitted with a flamethrower for anti-infantry operations; the Churchill ARK, an armored ramp carrier that could make mobile bridges to cross water hazards and difficult terrain; and the Churchill AVRE, a multi-use vehicle equipped with mine flails, Fascine rollers, explosive placers and a 290mm Spigot mortar for leveling buildings. In fact, the Churchill proved so versatile that late on in the war it was even converted into an Armored Personnel Carrier (APC), with engineers removing its turret completely. This variant was called the Churchill Kangaroo, (see photo below).

ENGINE
The Mk VII's engine was a Bedford, horizontally opposed, twin-six petrol engine capable of producing 350bhp at 2,200rpm. The average speed of the Churchill Mk VII was 12.7mph, significantly less than the Mk I due to increased armor thickness

A Churchill Kangaroo, the variant of the tank converted to be an Armored Personnel Carrier

WILLYS JEEP

The most iconic light transport vehicle of World War II, the Willys jeep was versatile, maneuverable and fast over uneven terrain

The first and most distinctive jeep ever built, the Willys jeep was designed in 1940 as part of a competition to provide the US Army with a new light transport vehicle for the impending World War II. It dictated light transport vehicle design for decades to come, only being phased out in the late Seventies. Light, adaptable and highly maneuverable, the Willys jeep in its various forms (MA, MB and post-war M38/M606) allowed allied forces to transport troops, munitions and injured soldiers to and from the front line quickly and efficiently.

Central to its effectiveness was its L134 2.2-liter engine, capable of producing 60hp at 4,000rpm. This granted the lightweight Willys (1,040kg) a top speed of 45mph and earned the engine the nickname of 'Go Devil' by Allied troops. The engine was controlled by a Warner T-84J three-speed synchromesh transmission, which provided three forward gears and one in reverse in a four-wheel drive setup, allowing for the jeep to easily traverse road, desert, scrub and jungle terrain.

The engine was forward-mounted to a lightweight steel chassis. This featured a foldable windscreen, slatted iron grille (later additions included a steel grated grille), and front frame cross-member for rigidity and damage mitigation. The chassis sat on top of a compact 80-inch wheelbase that was installed with leaf springs and shock absorbers (excellent for passage over bumpy ground), as well as fully hydraulic brakes on each of its four wheels (granting fantastic stopping power).

The Willys jeep was also prized for its high adaptability, with various different vehicle setups possible dependent on the mission role in question. Troop transport maximized passenger space, with extra seats at the rear, while as a mobile medical center the rear seats could be removed to make way for stretchers, medicines and operating equipment. The jeep could also be installed with various weapons platforms, including

The Willys' versatility was its greatest asset, allowing it to be used in a variety of roles

a rear-mounted 37mm cannon and array of different Browning M1917 machine guns.

While the Willys jeep was subsequently upgraded post-war with a larger engine (the F4-134 Hurricane), more durable transmission (Warner T-90) and a range of advanced instrumentation and electronics, it was eventually replaced in the late Seventies and early Eighties as larger, more armored vehicles like the Humvee became the military's primary troop transporters.

Willys could transport the injured on stretchers as the rear seats were removable

"THE WILLYS JEEP WAS PRIZED FOR ITS HIGH ADAPTABILITY, WITH VARIOUS DIFFERENT SETUPS POSSIBLE DEPENDENT ON MISSION ROLE"

WW II soldiers march alongside a Willys jeep towing a trailer

Willys MA jeep undergoing desert trials

INSTRUMENTATION

The Willys MB jeep was fitted with a 0-60 mph speedometer, 0-220 Fahrenheit temperature gauge, oil pressure monitor and map light

UNDER THE HOOD

THE COMPONENTS THAT MADE UP THIS EFFECTIVE WAR VEHICLE

CHASSIS

The jeep's chassis was lightweight and constructed from steel. It featured a foldable windscreen, stamped forward grille and U-shaped cross-member

2054718

WHEELBASE

The Willys MB wheelbase was 80 inches and featured leaf springs and shock absorbers, full hydraulic breaks on each wheel and a handbrake assembly at the rear of the transfer case

TRANSMISSION

The MB sported a Warner T-84J three-speed synchromesh transmission, with three forward gears of increasing speed and one in reverse. The MB was predominantly four-wheel drive

ENGINE

The Willys L134 engine powered the MB and was nicknamed the 'Go Devil', due to its power. The engine was 2.2 liters in size, could produce 60hp at 4,000rpm and featured an in-built oil filter, oil mesh, throat carburettor and manual choke

The engine bay of the Willys MB, clearly showing its L134, 'Go Devil' engine

WILLYS JEEP

CREW 3
CAPACITY 5
WEIGHT 2,293LB
LENGTH 131 INCHES
WIDTH 62 INCHES
HEIGHT 72 INCHES
ENGINE 4-CYLINDER, 2.2-LITER L134 PETROL
MAX HORSEPOWER 60HP @ 4,000RPM
MAX SPEED 45MPH
TRANSMISSION WARNER T-84J 3-SPEED SYNCHROMESH
PRODUCED 640,000

A Willys jeep of the US 3rd Infantry, Newfoundland, 1942. Note the large 37mm cannon and M1917 Browning machine gun

SU-76M
TANK DESTROYER

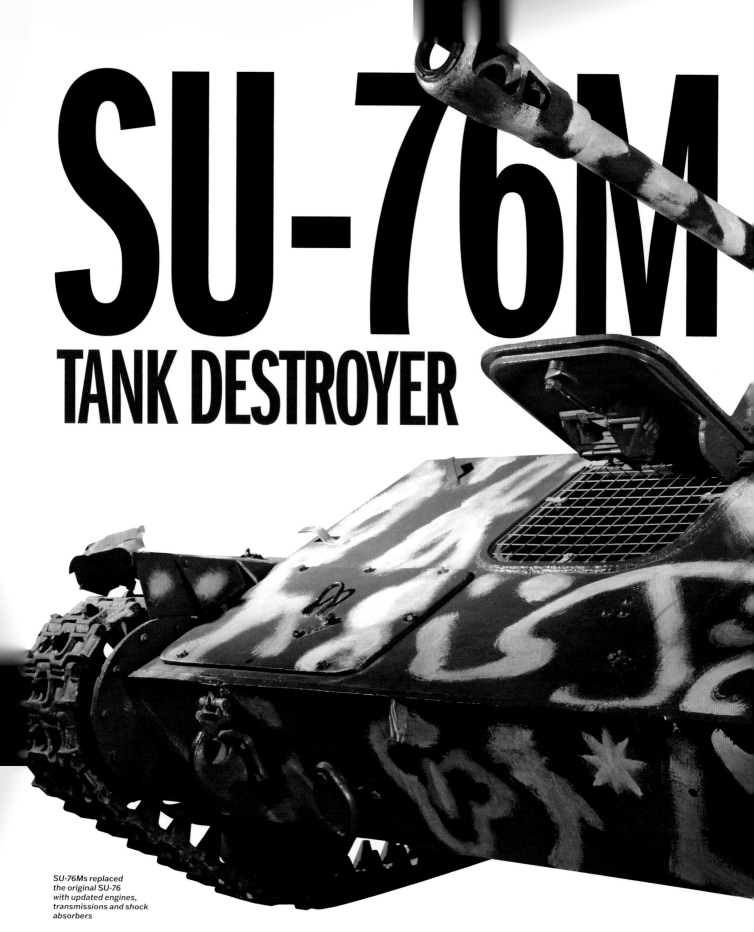

SU-76Ms replaced the original SU-76 with updated engines, transmissions and shock absorbers

Meet the tank killer that helped halt the German advance into Soviet lands and turn the tide of Russia's Great Patriotic War

If the First World War was the birth of tanks, the Second World War was the birth of tank killers. Used in high numbers by the Wehrmacht and Red Army (but not so much by the Allied powers), a field gun attached to a tank chassis would create a mobile heavy gun and an infantry support weapon in the field of battle. The SU-76M was the successor to the original SU-76 and was mass-produced by the USSR in an attempt to defeat the panzers that were advancing ever eastwards.

Production began in December 1942 and they became a triumph of Soviet handiwork. Hastily produced, they paled in

"THE SU-76M WAS MASS-PRODUCED BY THE USSR IN AN ATTEMPT TO DEFEAT THE FORMIDABLE RANKS OF PANZERS THAT WERE ADVANCING EVER EASTWARDS"

comparison with their German equivalents but their sheer numbers (over 12,500 were built) meant they could easily outflank any German advance. This was a factor in the reverse in fortunes of the Germans on the Eastern Front at the Battle of Kursk.

After the end of the war, the SU-76M model was used in the Korean War on the side of the Communist forces of North Korea until it was phased out by more modern vehicles

and methods of warfare. Even when they were replaced, many were stripped of their guns and remodeled into ammunition carriers and battlefield recovery vehicles. There were many different SU-76s in the Red Army. The SU-7B had a closed crew compartment while the SU-76P and SU-76I were based on the Soviet T-26 and German Panzer III. The design also set out the template for the ZSU-37, which became the Soviet self-propelled AA gun of choice.

SU-76Ms used their camouflage and the terrain to stealthily advance upon unwitting enemy tank divisions

Soviet soldiers hitch a ride on an SU-76M as they liberate a German town

SU-76M

COMMISSIONED: DECEMBER 1942
ORIGIN: USSR
LENGTH: 16FT
WIDTH: 9FT
ENGINE: 2X 85HP GAZ-203
CREW: 4
ARMOR: 35MM (FRONT), 16MM (SIDES)
SPEED: 27.3MPH
PRIMARY WEAPON: 1X 76.2MM ZIS-3 L/41 FIELD GUN
SECONDARY WEAPONS: DEGTYARYOV MACHINE GUN; CREW'S PERSONAL ARMS

76MM GUN

By 1942 the Soviets were taking the full brunt of the Nazi onslaught on the Eastern Front. The mass-produced T-34 tanks were effective but something more was needed to tilt the war in their favor. The decision was made to begin the production of so-called 'tank destroyers' that would halt the panzer advance.

The 76.2mm gun fared well against the Panzer III and IV but as stronger German tanks rolled onto the front, the SU-76M was reduced to an infantry support vehicle, as it could not penetrate the thick armor of the Tiger and Panther tanks. Some models of the SU-76 could also have anti-aircraft guns mounted instead and there was also a short-lived prototype with a 57mm armament as the Red Army tinkered with the tank-destroyer formula.

The 76.2mm gun was effective against the earlier Panzers but found it very difficult to puncture a Tiger's thick armor

The ZiS-3 76.2mm was taken from a Russian field gun and attached to a tank chassis

"THE MOST EFFECTIVE TACTIC WOULD BE TO FLANK A PANZER AND CATCH IT OFF GUARD WITH A STRIKE ON THE WEAKER ARMOR"

GAZ-203S ENGINE

The original SU-76 was powered by two GAZ-202 engines but they were replaced on the SU-76M with GAZ-203s due to issues with the transmission. Coupled with the loss of weight due to the open top, the engine and machinery within the SU-76 generally worked quite well.

They were the polar opposite of the German-made tank destroyers such as the Jagdtiger, which were more powerful but much fewer in number. The chassis of the SU-76M was taken from the Soviet T-70 tank, as this light tank was slowly being phased out by the Red Army. The model wasn't particularly popular with the crew due to its limited protection but it nevertheless assumed an important role within the USSR's forces.

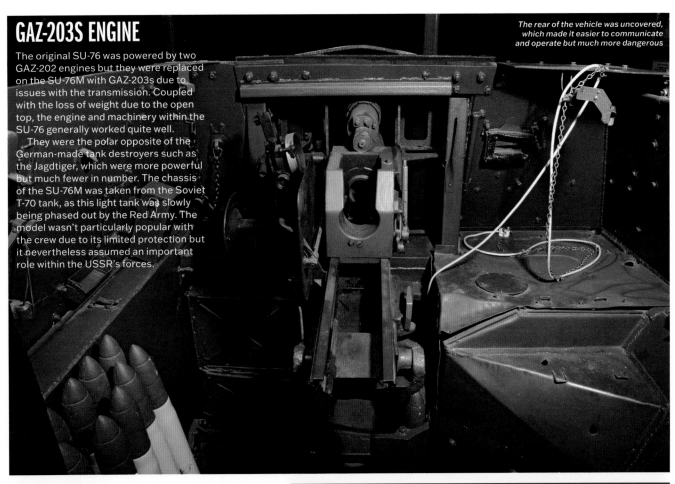

The rear of the vehicle was uncovered, which made it easier to communicate and operate but much more dangerous

35MM ARMOR

The tank killer's game was based on using camouflage and cover rather than going in all guns blazing. The most effective tactic would be to flank a panzer and catch it off-guard with a strike on the weaker armor at the side or rear. If the SU-76M was caught out in the open, it had 35mm armor on its front and 16mm on its sides. This armor was strengthened on the later SU-76Ms that served in the final months of the Second World War and the Korean War. Unlike a tank, the SU-76 was open at the back to allow the gunner and loader to communicate with other vehicles with hand signals. The downside to this was the lack of protection to the crew. This was rectified on several later designs but they never made it past the prototype stage.

The armor of the SU-76M wasn't famed for its thickness and could be pierced by machine gun fire

THE OTHER TANK KILLERS
THE SU-76M WASN'T THE ONLY VEHICLE ON THE BATTLEFIELD THAT WAS DESIGNED TO ELIMINATE TANKS

STURMGESCHÜTZ III GERMAN ▬
Based on the body of a Panzer III, the StuG III was the German equivalent of the SU-76M. It was employed in a defensive role and its 75mm gun could penetrate 85mm thick tank armor from over 3,280ft away.

M10 AMERICAN ▬
The M10s were based on Sherman M4A2 tanks and were employed in Western Europe in specialized tank destroyer battalions. The M10s had thick 37mm armor and were implemented into the Danish, Dutch and Belgian armies during the struggle against the Wehrmacht.

ARCHER BRITISH ▬
An unusual design, the Archer was born out of the British army's desire to create a mobile transport for its 17 pounder anti-tank gun. Despite being unable to fire when moving, the Archers proved successful and were in use until the Fifties.

JAGDTIGER GERMAN ▬
The heaviest tank killer of then all, the Jagdtiger was produced far too late to have any effect on the war. Only 80 of these 70-ton machines were made and they were constantly dogged with engine and fuel issues.

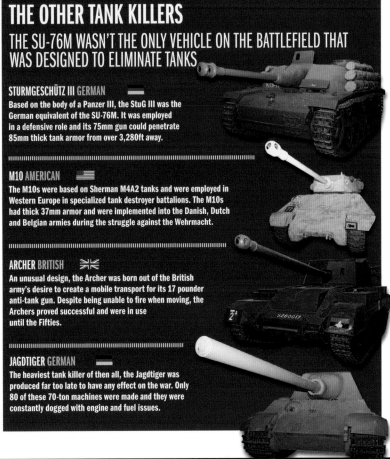

THE SU-76M IN THE FIELD

TANK MUSEUM WARDEN TOM MOORCROFT ON THE FAMOUS RUSSIAN TANK KILLER

WHAT ROLE DID THE VEHICLE HAVE WHEN DEPLOYED ON THE BATTLEFIELD?

It was mainly used for heavy suppressing fire and pursuing tanks. It is basically a mobile artillery gun. The difference between it and a tank is that a tank has a turret.

HOW DID IT STAND UP AGAINST THE FORMIDABLE GERMAN TIGER TANKS?

The SU-76, as the name says, has the smaller 76mm gun. It was later upgraded to an 85mm gun to combat the Tiger and Tiger II whose armor was far too thick to penetrate. Ideally this vehicle would be used against smaller tanks such as the Panzer III and Panzer IV.

WHAT WERE THE CONDITIONS LIKE INSIDE?

Pretty much the same as any tank but it's open at the back and is essentially a convertible! The loader and gunner would be on the rear while the driver sat below the gun at the front. It's based on the T-34 but it is actually quite dissimilar with its open roof.

WHAT TANK WAS IT MOST EFFECTIVE AGAINST?

Only the Germans and the Russians really used tank destroyers, as the UK and the USA preferred just using tanks. When used with tanks and machine guns, it could hold off an enemy advance. Even when enemy tanks weren't spotted, the SU-76 could be very effective as a camouflaged artillery gun against infantry before the main armored column arrived.

DID IT HAVE ANY FLAWS?

The problem with a tank destroyer is the limited movement of the gun, which can only aim up and down and not 360 degrees. If you want to fire left and right, you have to move the whole vehicle. When enemy convoys split up, an SU-76 could be easily outflanked. However, this vehicle is a very good example of Russian mechanical reliability. German tank killers such as the Jagdtiger were so complicated to build, by the time you've made one of them, you've made many SU-76s. They are very crude in their design but you just make as many as you can.

AFTER THE END OF THE KOREAN WAR, DID TANK KILLERS REALLY BECOME OBSOLETE?

Well, that argument has been going on throughout the history of the tank – is the tank really relevant? Personally, if the enemy has tanks, you're always going to need tanks yourself in order to lead a counterattack. In the territory of the Korean War, you can't really use tanks in urban warfare but they are still very effective in open fields as long as you don't get bogged down!

Below: The rear of the SU-76M was open to the elements, giving the gunner and loader little to no protection

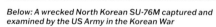

Below: A wrecked North Korean SU-76M captured and examined by the US Army in the Korean War

The SU-76M wasn't overly popular with its crews and was called 'Suka' meaning 'The Bitch'

TANK DESTROYERS IN MODERN WARFARE

ARE TANK KILLERS RELEVANT IN TODAY'S CONFLICTS?

After the Second World War, Nazi Germany went through a mass disarmament process and the USSR sheltered behind its impenetrable Iron Curtain. So, what happened to the tank destroyer? The SU-76M model was sold in large swathes to North Korea but as tanks got stronger and wars became more covert in nature, the role of the tank destroyer began to diminish.

Some still remain today, although they look different to the World War Two vintage. Rather than installing field guns, missile launchers are now a much more effective way of laying waste to armored tanks on the battlefield. Although lightly armored, the missile's guided systems allow the tank destroyer to strike from a reasonable distance.

"AS TANKS GOT STRONGER AND WARS BECAME MORE COVERT IN NATURE, THE ROLE OF THE TANK DESTROYER BEGAN TO DIMINISH"

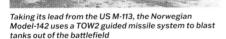

Taking its lead from the US M-113, the Norwegian Model-142 uses a TOW2 guided missile system to blast tanks out of the battlefield

This British tank destroyer was introduced in 1975 and saw service in the Gulf War. Its Swingfire missiles have a range of 13,120ft

Breaking away from the traditional look, this was the first guided missile anti-tank vehicle to be produced when it made its debut in 1962

Though highly effective during their heyday, tank destroyers have largely been phased out of modern armies

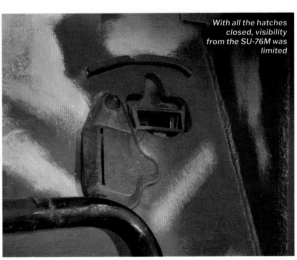

With all the hatches closed, visibility from the SU-76M was limited

The Tank Museum; Alamy; Getty

A DAY IN THE LIFE OF A TANK DESTROYER CREW

WHAT WAS IT LIKE TO SPEND 24 HOURS WITH A RED ARMY TANK KILLER SQUAD?

With the might of the German Armored Division racing east, the life of a Soviet tank crew was a daunting one. The crew would be composed of three or four people: a driver, a gunner, a loader and occasionally an extra pair of hands to help with the running of the vehicle. As the rear of the SU-76M was uncovered, both the loader and the gunner were open to the worst of the Russian winter and were unprotected from gunfire. The only good news about an uncovered rear was that the blast radius from a German Panzerschreck would not be as severe. The mobility of the vehicle was key to avoid as much fire as possible as well as getting in close and getting a better shot at the enemy panzers. Long-distance shots wouldn't have penetrated the armor, plus a shot on the side or the rear of a Tiger or Panther would do much more damage. The fuel capacity was around 101 gallons of fuel so the tank destroyer could stay in action for a good amount of time. As well as battlefields like Kursk, the SU-76M was useful in urban environments as the Red Army pursued the Wehrmacht through the cities of Eastern Europe. The 76.2mm field gun could blast through buildings and strongholds while the open rear allowed the crew to hop off and introduce the enemy to the full brunt of the PPSH-41 submachine gun. Overall, the SU-76M was an integral feature of the Eastern Front for the Allies. The vehicle revitalized what was a redundant tank chassis and was immensely useful to the Red Army in what they knew as the 'Great Patriotic War'.

A SU-76M crew consults a map and discusses tactics on their advance through Hungary in the Second World War

CHARTING THE EVOLUTION OF SELF-PROPELLED ANTI-TANK WEAPONS

WHERE DID THE USSR GO AFTER THE SU-76M?

At the end of the Second World War, a new threat faced forces and civilians alike: nuclear weaponry. With the Cold War looming, members of NATO preferred to concentrate on the idea that ground forces and nuclear weaponry would be used separately, in separate theaters. The USSR was more pragmatic, reasoning that even within Europe, it was likely that any major conflict would see the use of both, probably within range of each other. Realizing that troops would need protection from radiation and that anti-tank ordnance would need to move faster in order to be effective, they changed the role of anti-tank weaponry from defensive to offensive, increasing their mobility and giving rise to powerful anti-tank missiles launched from faster vehicles.

STURMGESCHÜTZ III GERMAN
Based on the body of a Panzer III, the StuG III was the German equivalent of the SU-76M. It was employed in a defensive role and its 75mm gun could penetrate 85mm thick tank armor from over 3,280ft away.

SU-100
Even the SU-85 couldn't quite puncture the armor of the mighty Tigers so yet another upgrade was produced with a 100mm anti-tank gun. They came into use in late 1944 and were part of the final push into Germany.

SU-152
Utilizing a huge 152mm gun, the SU-152 was essentially a howitzer placed on top of a KV-1 heavy tank. It had the potential to knock out the strongest enemy tanks and was so powerful it was used against fortifications.

ASU-85
After the war, the tank destroyer morphed into what is known as a self-propelled gun. The ASU-85 was one such development, and has been replaced by new models such as the BMD-1 and BTR-D, which is still used today.

SU-76 VARIATIONS
THE SU-76M WAS SO POPULAR THAT IT CAME IN A VARIETY OF FORMS AND EVOLUTIONS DURING ITS LIFESPAN

OSU-76
This experimental version of the SU-76M was modeled on a T-60 tank rather than a T-70 but never made it off the Red Army's production line.

SU-76
Building on the good work made by the OSU-76, this version was based on a T-70 tank and was the precursor to the SU-76M.

SU-76B
An upgrade on the main model, only a few of these were produced. This tank killer gave the driver and gunner more protection with a fully enclosed crew compartment.

SU-76I
Over 1,000 of these hybrid versions were created during the war from converted StuG III captured from the Wehrmacht.

"THE 76.2MM FIELD BLAST THROUGH BUI AND STRONGHOLDS, OPEN REAR ALLOWED CREW DEPLOYMENT"

A jack of all trades, the Humvee can be configured to perform many roles

A snorkel and raised exhaust make the Humvee a great amphibious vehicle

HUMVEE

The high-mobility multipurpose wheeled vehicle (HMMWV) roars off the production line ready for action

Designed to replace several outdated American military vehicles, the high-mobility multipurpose wheeled vehicle, or Humvee, has been in production since 1985. Originally intended as a light utility vehicle, there have been more than 20 variants of this highly customizable, modular platform. Serving over 40 nations, around 200,000 Humvees have been built to date. Able to carry and deploy almost anything, from fully armed troops to anti-aircraft missiles, the Humvee is an open-topped scout vehicle, an armored personnel carrier, ambulance, a TOW missile launcher, a communication center, a heavy machine gun platform and whatever else the situation requires.

The latest models are unrivaled in their off-road capability, and are based around a 6.5-liter V8 Turbo diesel engine which produces 190 brake horsepower and 380 pounds force per foot of torque. This power is sent to all four wheels through an electronically controlled four-speed automatic gearbox, using a series of differentials. The drivetrain is rather unconventional as the wheels themselves contain portal-geared hubs, which not only double the torque generated, but due to the offset driveshaft inputs, enable the vehicle's ground clearance to be significantly higher than a regular center axle

would allow. This innovative drivetrain, coupled with independent suspension and 37-inch tires, allow the Humvee to travel at 70 miles per hour or to climb slopes of 60 percent – though some Humvees have been seen to climb near-vertical walls! The internal environment is fully air conditioned, while a deep-water fording kit allows the vehicle to cross rivers almost completely submerged. These capabilities, combined with design features such as the sturdy chassis, corrosion resistance plus high commonality and interchangeable parts, enable the Humvee to be flexible, dependable and rugged even in the harshest of environments.

The turret can be fitted with weapons for all kinds of combat situation

ARMOR OPTIONS

Since the Humvee was first introduced, soldiers have demanded increasingly more protection from it. Early versions had fabric doors and no roof, but the demands of conflicts in Somalia, Iraq and Afghanistan demonstrated the need for improved armor. Many improvised solutions have been tried in the field in recent years, including sandbags and welding scrap metal to the chassis. However, heavily armored versions are now available from the factory, as are retrofit kits, which include under-body plates, heavy doors, armored seats, weapon shields and numerous other additions. The latest iterations offer the crew protection from assault rifle bullets, some air-burst artillery, and up to 12 pounds of explosives, thanks to thick steel armor, energy-absorbing coatings and mounting, and reinforced glass. All of this comes at a price, though, with many Humvees carrying 2,000–4,000 pounds of armor, which can only be taken in place of cargo and equipment. Work is now underway to make the Humvee more resistant to buried explosives, as in its current state, the large flat floor is not effective against these.

INSIDE THE HUMVEE

WE TEAR DOWN ONE OF THESE TOUGH VEHICLES TO FIND OUT WHAT MAKES IT SO
WELL SUITED TO OFF-ROAD COMBAT

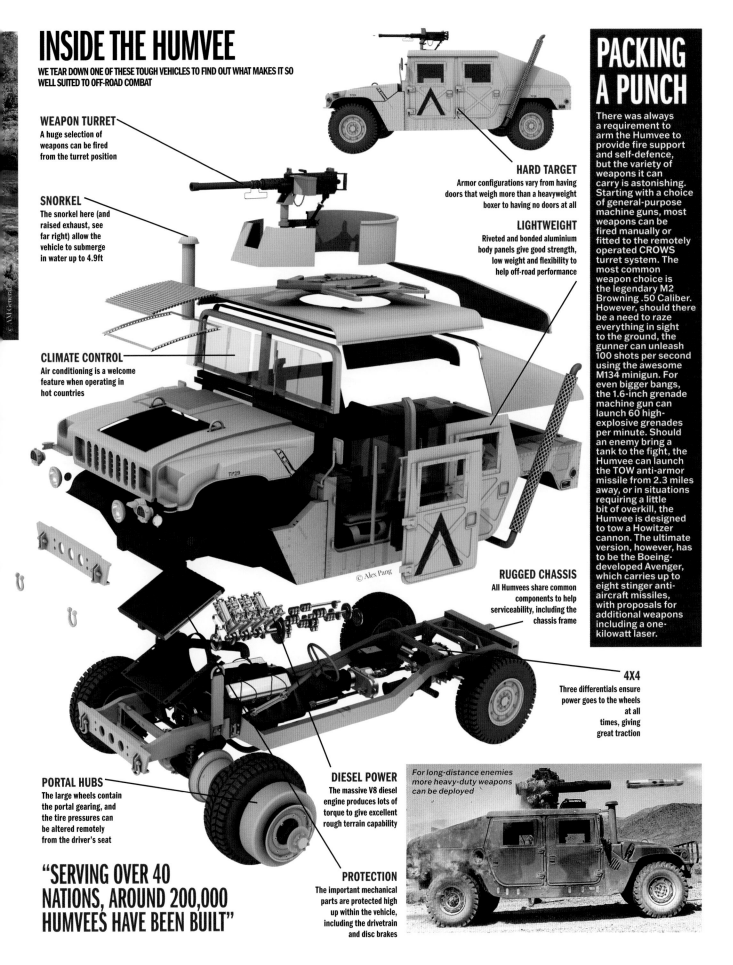

© AM General

© Alex Pang

WEAPON TURRET
A huge selection of
weapons can be fired
from the turret position

SNORKEL
The snorkel here (and
raised exhaust, see
far right) allow the
vehicle to submerge
in water up to 4.9ft

CLIMATE CONTROL
Air conditioning is a welcome
feature when operating in
hot countries

HARD TARGET
Armor configurations vary from having
doors that weigh more than a heavyweight
boxer to having no doors at all

LIGHTWEIGHT
Riveted and bonded aluminium
body panels give good strength,
low weight and flexibility to
help off-road performance

RUGGED CHASSIS
All Humvees share common
components to help
serviceability, including the
chassis frame

4X4
Three differentials ensure
power goes to the wheels
at all
times, giving
great traction

PORTAL HUBS
The large wheels contain
the portal gearing, and
the tire pressures can
be altered remotely
from the driver's seat

DIESEL POWER
The massive V8 diesel
engine produces lots of
torque to give excellent
rough terrain capability

PROTECTION
The important mechanical
parts are protected high
up within the vehicle,
including the drivetrain
and disc brakes

"SERVING OVER 40 NATIONS, AROUND 200,000 HUMVEES HAVE BEEN BUILT"

PACKING A PUNCH

There was always
a requirement to
arm the Humvee to
provide fire support
and self-defence,
but the variety of
weapons it can
carry is astonishing.
Starting with a choice
of general-purpose
machine guns, most
weapons can be
fired manually or
fitted to the remotely
operated CROWS
turret system. The
most common
weapon choice is
the legendary M2
Browning .50 Caliber.
However, should there
be a need to raze
everything in sight
to the ground, the
gunner can unleash
100 shots per second
using the awesome
M134 minigun. For
even bigger bangs,
the 1.6-inch grenade
machine gun can
launch 60 high-
explosive grenades
per minute. Should
an enemy bring a
tank to the fight, the
Humvee can launch
the TOW anti-armor
missile from 2.3 miles
away, or in situations
requiring a little
bit of overkill, the
Humvee is designed
to tow a Howitzer
cannon. The ultimate
version, however, has
to be the Boeing-
developed Avenger,
which carries up to
eight stinger anti-
aircraft missiles,
with proposals for
additional weapons
including a one-
kilowatt laser.

For long-distance enemies more heavy-duty weapons can be deployed

SUPER-SMART COMBAT TANKS

A new fleet of futuristic and highly adaptable armored attack vehicles is looking to revolutionize how conflicts are fought on the 21st-century battlefield

For decades tank design has been held in the vice-like grip of the 'Iron Triangle', a design mantra that states that any tank – in order to succeed on the battlefield – needs to be built on the sturdy columns of firepower, protection and mobility. The perfect tank, it was deemed, would be a seamless combination of these three key qualities – a machine that could withstand a host of armor-piercing shells, transport its crew both quickly and safely across a war-torn battlefield, and then deliver a series of explosive shells into enemy structures and vehicles.

Today's most advanced tanks are testament to the Iron Triangle – just look at the awesome firepower and armor

delivered by the M1 Abrams main battle tank – delivering, in varying degrees of success, heavily armed and armored mobile fortresses capable of leveling city blocks and boosting an army's odds in any conflict they are deployed in.

However, times are changing. The modern 21st-century battlefield differs radically from that experienced in the mid-20th century when much of today's top armor was conceived. The theater of war in the present is more fluid, fast-moving and interconnected than ever before, demanding armies react quickly and efficiently to any intelligence gathered to stay on top. In essence, intelligence and adaptability are now central to any armored fighting vehicle, and

these qualities are rapidly reshaping the Iron Triangle into an 'Iron Pentagon' with which any new build must comply if it's to be an out-and-out success.

Here we take a close look at three of the most notable armored fighting vehicles that are being constructed following the Iron Pentagon principle. These mighty machines not only offer bucketloads of armor and smart munitions, but also deliver advanced electronic architectures, near-omniscient sensors, super-fast internet networks, modular structures to adapt to any situation, plus revolutionary propulsion units.

So, strap yourself in and pay attention, as knowledge is power – and boy do these tanks go a long way to prove it!

ASCOD SV: THE SCOUT

The Specialist Vehicle (SV) is the British Army's new, medium-weight armored fighting vehicle built on General Dynamics' ASCOD platform. The platform is designed to fulfil various roles that are currently handled by one specialized vehicle. As such, the SV is able to undertake all the diverse roles of these traditional vehicles, replacing them and reducing both costs and training timescales.

This is possible for two main reasons. The SV's modular architecture allows a number of specialized vehicles to be generated from one common base platform (CBP). So, the SV can deliver some 17 variants, including the Scout reconnaissance variant, armored personnel carrier, direct fire light tank, command and control vehicle, ambulance, through to recovery and repair engineering vehicles.

Another reason the SV is the 'Swiss Army knife' of the tank world is its integration of an advanced open electronic architecture system. This allows the SV's base vehicle to communicate with any systems unique to its specialized variants, enabling full sensor suite integration and easy control by its operator. It also helps manage the intelligence that can be captured, analyzed and stored by the SV, which can be transferred over the latest Ethernet network to the rest of the battlegroup – be they on foot, in other vehicles or at base.

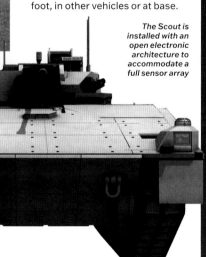

The Scout is installed with an open electronic architecture to accommodate a full sensor array

ANATOMY OF THE SCOUT SV

DISCOVER THE FEATURES THAT MAKE THE SCOUT A REVOLUTIONARY PIECE OF TECHNOLOGY

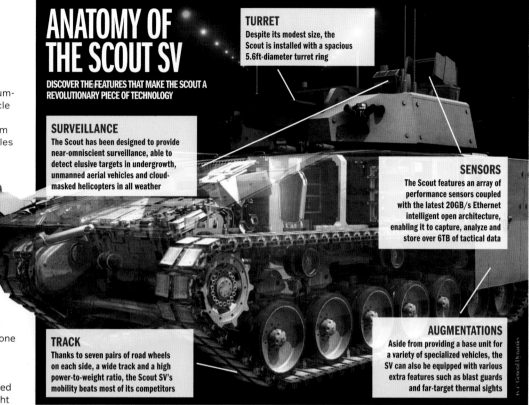

TURRET
Despite its modest size, the Scout is installed with a spacious 5.6ft-diameter turret ring

SURVEILLANCE
The Scout has been designed to provide near-omniscient surveillance, able to detect elusive targets in undergrowth, unmanned aerial vehicles and cloud-masked helicopters in all weather

SENSORS
The Scout features an array of performance sensors coupled with the latest 20GB/s Ethernet intelligent open architecture, enabling it to capture, analyze and store over 6TB of tactical data

TRACK
Thanks to seven pairs of road wheels on each side, a wide track and a high power-to-weight ratio, the Scout SV's mobility beats most of its competitors

AUGMENTATIONS
Aside from providing a base unit for a variety of specialized vehicles, the SV can also be equipped with various extra features such as blast guards and far-target thermal sights

© General Dynamics

SCOUT SV

WEIGHT 34 TONS SCOUT VARIANT (UP TO 42 TONS WITH UPGRADES)
ENGINE MTU V8 DIESEL
POWER 805HP
TOP SPEED 44MPH
ARMAMENT 1 X 1.2IN CTAI CANNON; 1 X 0.3IN COAXIAL MACHINE GUN
ARMOR 360° PROTECTION USING LATEST PROVEN MODULAR ARMOR

"THE SV'S MODULAR ARCHITECTURE ALLOWS A NUMBER OF SPECIALIZED VEHICLES TO BE GENERATED OFF THE BACK OF ONE COMMON BASE PLATFORM"

5 Facts about SMART TANKS

FRES
The MOD's Future Rapid Effect System (FRES) project awarded a Specialist Vehicle contract to General Dynamics for the ASCOD AFV in March 2010 – the first of the program.

GLOBAL APPEAL
The CV90 is already in operation in Denmark, the Netherlands, Norway, Finland, Switzerland and Sweden. Its latest iteration is currently in evaluation in Canada, the US and Poland.

PRIVATE EYES
BAE-Northrop Grumman's new Ground Combat Vehicle uses a hybrid electric drive (HED) for propulsion, delivering a top speed of 44mph as well as enhanced efficiency.

ECONOMY BOOST
By value, 80 percent of the Scout SV vehicles will be completed in the UK, with 70 percent of the supply chain companies UK-based, boosting the British defence industry.

ARMADILLO
The latest build standard for the CV90 is the Armadillo. This has been redesigned to focus on commonality between tank variants and is modular for easy configuration switching.

MODULAR MAYHEM

ONE OF THE SV'S MOST IMPRESSIVE QUALITIES IS ITS MODULAR DESIGN, ALLOWING IT TO BE CUSTOMIZED EXTENSIVELY

Thanks to its common base platform (CBP) and advanced electronic architecture, SV variants will be able to handle a host of different roles on the battlefield. For example, the SV family offers a light tank, anti-aircraft and missile gun station, repair and recovery vehicle, command and communication vehicle and ambulance among other vehicles. Each of these

variations can be outfitted to fulfil roles laid out in the British Ministry of Defence's Future Rapid Effect System (FRES) program, a project designed to create a large fleet of network-enabled, cross-spectrum armored fighting vehicles. For example, the final phase of the development will also see a bridge layer and heavy-lifting vehicle developed.

CV90120: THE TANK KILLER

There is no escaping the CV90120's primary purpose: that of delivering a vehicle that offers the penetrative stopping power of a main battle tank, but with a weight, mobility and sensor suite comparable to a smaller and lighter specialist vehicle. And indeed it delivers, bringing the colossal Rheinmetall LLR/L47 4.7-inch anti-cannon to the battlefield, a gun that no armored vehicle in the world can withstand if a clean shot is landed. What's more exciting, however, is its revolutionary new electronic architecture and systems, as well as its unique ADAPTIV cloaking device.

The ADAPTIV system (see the 'Real-life invisibility cloak' section below for an explanation of how it works) enables the tank to cloak itself over the infrared spectrum from any surveillance radars, accurately mimicking other less dangerous vehicles – therefore supplying misinformation to enemies. It can even vanish all together, with the system drastically reducing its signature at

long and medium ranges. No other system like this is currently on the market worldwide and, when you factor in that ADAPTIV is already being used in the field, then its game-changing qualities really shine through.

Another real high point of this next-generation fighter is its impressive suite of electronic survival features. These include laser, radar and missile approach warning systems, various multispectral, aerosol active countermeasures, a top-mounted attack radar that can identify precision anti-tank munitions, and a detailed vehicle information system (VIS). The latter supplies crew members with a vast array of battlefield information and intelligence, as well as various system parameters.

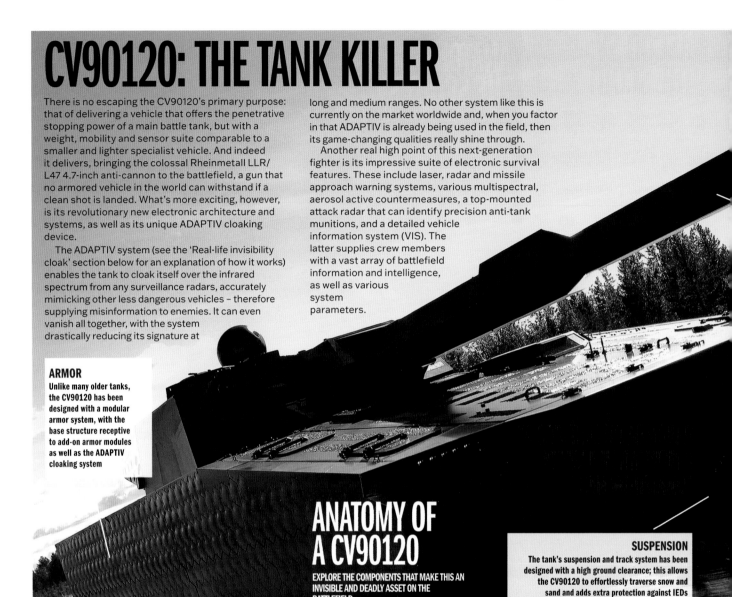

ARMOR
Unlike many older tanks, the CV90120 has been designed with a modular armor system, with the base structure receptive to add-on armor modules as well as the ADAPTIV cloaking system

ANATOMY OF A CV90120
EXPLORE THE COMPONENTS THAT MAKE THIS AN INVISIBLE AND DEADLY ASSET ON THE BATTLEFIELD

SUSPENSION
The tank's suspension and track system has been designed with a high ground clearance; this allows the CV90120 to effortlessly traverse snow and sand and adds extra protection against IEDs

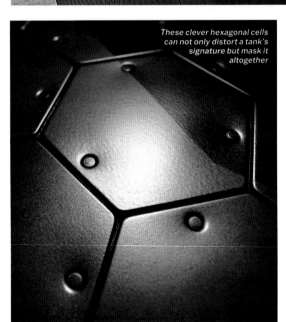

These clever hexagonal cells can not only distort a tank's signature but mask it altogether

THE REAL-LIFE INVISIBILITY CLOAK

THE CV90120 IS HARDWIRED WITH BAE'S ADAPTIV ARMOR, A REVOLUTIONARY NEW ELECTRICAL CAMOUFLAGE SYSTEM

The ADAPTIV system works by using lightweight, metallic, hexagonal pixels to cover a vehicle's armor, which themselves are powered by the unit's internal electrical system. The pixels are then individually heated and/or cooled using semi-conductors to either remove the tank's heat/radar signature entirely from surveillance radars – making it invisible to the enemy – or mimic the heat signature of another vehicle. As such, the CV90120 tank can quickly and quietly assume the appearance of a 4x4 and have its true threat remain undetected.

Interestingly, the ADAPTIV technology also allows the host vehicle to mimic the textures of other objects, minimizing its radar signature even further and enabling it to appear like a range of inanimate natural objects, such as a large rock.

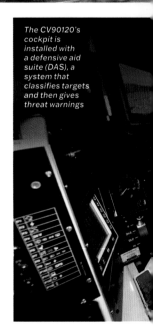

The CV90120's cockpit is installed with a defensive aid suite (DAS), a system that classifies targets and then gives threat warnings

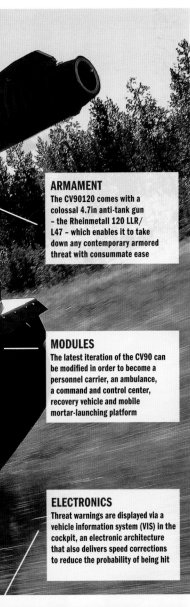

GCV: THE MOBILE FORTRESS

BAE Systems-Northrop Grumman's brand-new Ground Combat Vehicle (GCV) has been designed to provide the right mix of capabilities to adequately tackle the 21st-century battlefield, while also innovating in its delivery of cost-effectiveness over its scheduled 40-year life span. As such, the GCV has been designed to replace existing armored personnel carriers and light tanks, while also providing a modular common chassis from which future specialist vehicles can be evolved and produced.

The GCV features an adaptive platform built around a space-efficient steel core hull (the vehicle can carry a full squad of nine soldiers), an unmanned turret equipped with a one-inch autocannon and coaxial machine gun, and a cutting-edge hybrid electric drive (HED) propulsion unit. This smart tank can also boast an integrated C4ISR electronic network, including embedded intelligence, surveillance and reconnaissance assets in order to connect personnel to varied information sources – a vital asset in modern warfare.

The propulsion unit is the real star of the show though, offering exceptional force protection and mobility in such a lightweight vehicle. The benefits are marked: a 20 percent saving on fuel, 50 percent fewer moving parts, 60 percent reduction in total volume and increased on-board power delivery capabilities. Indeed, a standout feature of the vehicle is its ability to generate its own power even when stationary, a move intended to ready the GCV for the ongoing evolution of its systems.

ARMAMENT
The CV90120 comes with a colossal 4.7in anti-tank gun – the Rheinmetall 120 LLR/L47 – which enables it to take down any contemporary armored threat with consummate ease

MODULES
The latest iteration of the CV90 can be modified in order to become a personnel carrier, an ambulance, a command and control center, recovery vehicle and mobile mortar-launching platform

ELECTRONICS
Threat warnings are displayed via a vehicle information system (VIS) in the cockpit, an electronic architecture that also delivers speed corrections to reduce the probability of being hit

GCV

WEIGHT 140,000LB
RANGE 186MI
ENGINE HYBRID ELECTRIC DRIVE (HED)
POWER 1,044KW (1,400HP)
TOP SPEED 44MPH
ARMAMENT 1 X 1IN AUTOCANNON; 1 X 0.3IN COAXIAL MACHINE GUN

ANATOMY OF A GCV

DISCOVER A FEW REASONS WHY THE GROUND COMBAT VEHICLE IS SET TO BE WIDELY ADOPTED BY ARMIES WORLDWIDE

The GCV's use of a hybrid electric engine means it will have a 30-40-year life span

ARMAMENT
Despite its small size, the GCV is equipped with both a 1in autocannon and 0.3in coaxial machine gun, as well as an independent missile launcher operated by the vehicle's commander

PROPULSION
The GCV's hybrid electric drive engine delivers a 20 percent reduction in fuel consumption over legacy vehicles, as well as a 50 percent reduction in moving parts, essentially offering greater reliability

SUSPENSION
A lightweight and agile in-arm hydropneumatic suspension system consisting of seven road wheels and a 25in-wide track delivers excellent mobility across difficult terrain

SEA

HMS MEDUSA

88 Decades on, the boat that led the D-Day assault has been restored

HMS BELFAST

HMS WARRIOR

SUBMARINE HISTORY

HMS ALLIANCE

WARSHIPS

HOW THE NAVY OF THE FUTURE WILL RULE THE WAVES

Despite what the popular board game suggests, naval warfare isn't as easy as shouting a series of coordinates until the enemy's vessel is obliterated. A real-life game of battleships is all about military planning, precision and firepower.

Early battleships launched during the late 19th and early 20th century carried enormous guns capable of launching projectiles across the ocean surface to targets thousands of miles away. To defend themselves against enemy ships with equal firepower, they needed to be heavily armored too, with thick steel plates encasing their huge hulls.

During World War I, battleships became dominant naval weapons. Prior to the Great War, Germany challenged the Royal Navy as the most powerful fighting fleet; Britain hit back with the revolutionary HMS Dreadnought, kick-starting a naval arms race. However, by the outbreak of World War II, superior aircraft and submarine weapons had rendered the battleship obsolete, enabling the aircraft carrier to seize its position as capital ship of the fleet.

Navies could now attack targets within a much greater range than existing naval guns could reach, simply by sending out aircraft to deliver the devastating firepower instead. As a result, the role of warships became much more about close-range combat, with destroyers and cruisers carrying fewer and smaller guns, enabling them to be much lighter and more easily maneuverable when seeking out enemy targets.

Today, navies have an assortment of warships that they can call upon to tackle any situation, whether it's providing security for other vessels, responding to humanitarian disasters or attacking an enemy submarine hidden beneath the water. As new ships are developed, speed, efficiency and cost-effectiveness are key, with increased automation helping to shrink crew sizes.

For fleets of the future, only a few crew members may be needed on board, as computers, drones and unmanned boats carry out the difficult and dangerous duties instead. Advancements in technology could also bring back battleship-level firepower, with electromagnetic railguns and even laser weapons replacing heavier, more expensive firearms in the navy arsenal.

If these visions for future navy vessels come true, it could be even harder to catch up with, let alone sink, your opponent's ship in D7, before they fire their laser at your aircraft carrier in B10.

"FOR FLEETS OF THE FUTURE, ONLY A FEW CREW MEMBERS ARE NEEDED ON BOARD, AS COMPUTERS, DRONES AND UNMANNED BOATS CARRY OUT THE DANGEROUS DUTIES"

MEET THE FLEET

*Not to scale

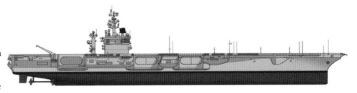

Aircraft carrier
These enormous airbases at sea are equipped with a flight deck for launching and landing short-range aircraft wherever they are needed

Cruiser
The second largest warships after aircraft carriers, cruisers have guided missile systems for taking out targets above, below or on the waves

Destroyer
These are slightly smaller, and therefore more agile than cruisers, and can provide protection from a variety of targets

Frigate
Designed mainly to hunt submarines, frigates are generally smaller than destroyers and are used to protect other warships and merchant convoys

Corvette
The navies of countries bordering small seas instead of large oceans often use small, lightly-armed corvettes to patrol their coasts

Submarine
These stealthy underwater vessels are silent hunters capable of surveillance and reconnaissance missions, as well as launching missiles

Amphibious assault ship
With a primary objective to get troops and their equipment to shore, these vessels can launch helicopters and other amphibious landing craft

Illustrations by Tom Connell/Art Agency

THE FUTURE OF WARSHIPS

What will naval fleets look like in the year 2050?

The Royal Navy has asked this very question, challenging young British scientists and engineers to design the fleet of the future. Their vision is the Dreadnought 2050 concept, a high-tech trimaran vessel built for speed, stability and efficiency. Named after the 1906 HMS Dreadnought, which was also a revolutionary vessel in its day, the sleek ship is almost fully automated, cutting today's crews of 200 down to 50 or 100 members.

Renewable energy technology could also give the ship unlimited range, allowing it to sail the world without stopping to refuel, and advanced weapons will enable immense firepower in battle. While some of the technologies envisioned for the Dreadnought 2050 are not yet achievable, others could realistically be incorporated into future designs, lowering the cost and manpower needed for the next generation of warships.

THE DREADNOUGHT 2050 CONCEPT
THE ROYAL NAVY'S PLANS FOR A HIGH-TECH WARSHIP OF THE FUTURE

Disarming technique
The tether is made from cryogenically cooled carbon nanotubes that can transmit power to the quadcopter's laser weapon and knock out enemy aircraft

Tethered drone
Instead of a conventional mast, a quadcopter carrying sensors such as radar is tethered above the ship

The flight deck's hangar can hold weaponized drones and a helicopter

See-through shell

Flight deck
The extendable flight deck at the back of the ship can be used to launch unmanned aerial vehicles (UAVs) equipped with weapons

3D printing
If additional UAVs are needed, they can be constructed on board the ship using 3D printing technology

Hypersonic missiles
Tubes running along the sides of the ship carry hypersonic missiles that can travel at over five times the speed of sound

A garage area at the stern of the ship holds a fleet of smaller boats

FLOODABLE GARAGE

Beneath the extendable flight deck and its fleet of drones is a garage full of even more specialist craft. These include unmanned underwater vehicles (UUVs) that can be used to detect mines on the ocean floor, and amphibious vessels used to transport troops to and from the shore for raiding missions. When the door of the garage is opened at sea, water floods in to submerge the lower level, transforming it into a platform from which these craft can be launched and recovered. A 'moon pool' – or small hole in the floor of the garage – also enables submersibles to be

THE STATISTICS...

DREADNOUGHT 2050

Length: 508ft	
Beam (width): 121ft	
Top speed: 57mph	
Crew: 50-100	
Range: Potentially unlimited	

HOLOGRAPHIC COMMAND CENTER

The days of pushing model ships around a map are long gone, as future naval operations will be planned using a 3D holographic command table. Located in the operations room at the heart of the ship, the table will allow commanders to rotate and zoom in to the hologram for a closer look at specific areas of the battlefield, which in reality can be thousands of miles away. Banks of 2D multi-functional displays can also be used to present and transmit data in real-time, while 'Google Glass-like' walls overlay additional information on a 360-degree view of the ship's surroundings.

"A HIGH-TECH TRIMARAN VESSEL BUILT FOR SPEED, STABILITY AND EFFICIENCY"

The ship's railgun uses electromagnetism to propel its projectiles

Tough exterior
The hull is coated in graphene, a strong yet lightweight material that will reduce drag for faster sailing

Torpedo bubbles
Tubes in the outrigger hulls contain torpedoes that can travel at 345mph, as they are encased in a bubble of gas that reduces friction

ELECTROMAGNETIC RAILGUN

Located on the ship's bow is a high-powered railgun that uses electromagnetic effects instead of explosive chemical propellants. The US Navy's current prototype railgun can fire projectiles at speeds of over Mach 7 (5,371mph), using kinetic energy rather than more conventional explosives to inflict damage and destroy the target.

Armature

Opposing magnetic fields
The current creates a magnetic field around each rail, one running clockwise and the other counter-clockwise

Positive rail

Projectile

Negative rail

Third magnetic field
A third magnetic field running perpendicular to the rails is created around the armature

Electric current
An electric current is passed up the positive rail, across the armature, and back down the negative rail

Aim and fire
The force propels the armature forward, firing the projectile towards its target

Lorentz force
The electric current and magnetic field interact to create what is known as Lorentz force, which accelerates the projectile

NEXT-GEN AIRCRAFT CARRIERS

Meet the colossal new centerpiece of the US Navy fleet

Aircraft carriers are often the capital ships of a nation's navy, helping the air and maritime forces work together to project air power worldwide. The US Navy currently has ten enormous nuclear-powered supercarriers in its fleet but a long-overdue upgrade is on its way. The first of the new Ford-class carriers, the USS Gerald R Ford, is currently undergoing the final phases of construction and testing, and is set to join the Navy's fleet in 2017. The USS Gerald R Ford, also known as CVN 78, will be similar in size to its predecessor Nimitz-class ships, but as the first aircraft carrier to be completely

designed using 3D computer modeling, it will be lighter, cheaper and more powerful. Increased automation will mean between 500 to 900 fewer crew members will be needed on board and for the first time, air conditioning will be available throughout the ship, making life at sea more comfortable. The carrier can hold up to 90 aircraft at a time, but instead of launching them using the steam-powered catapults found on modern day ships, an electromagnetic launch system will be used to fire them into the air. This works a lot like a railgun but uses an aircraft as the projectile.

The USS General R Ford's command center, known as the 'island', sits on the flight deck

"IT'S THE FIRST AIRCRAFT CARRIER TO BE COMPLETELY DESIGNED USING 3D COMPUTER MODELING"

The USS Gerald R Ford will be capable of loading weapons and launch aircraft faster than ever before

---

The final weight of the ship will be over

90,000 TONS

the equivalent of

4OO

STATUES OF LIBERTY

AROUND **200,000 GALLONS**

of paint will be needed to cover the ship, enough to cover

THE WHITE HOUSE

350 TIMES

---

10 million

feet of electrical cable will be installed on board, enough to reach the INTERNATIONAL SPACE STATION almost

8 times over

---

220 AIRCRAFT

can be deployed from the flight deck each day

25 %

more than from the Nimitz-class ships

Reduced manning and maintenance will save the US Navy more than

$4 billion

(APPROX £2.6 BILLION)

over the ship's

50 YEAR LIFESPAN

The heaviest component of the ship weighs

1,026 TONS

AS MUCH AS

6 BOEING 747 JETS

It was hoisted into place by a

1,050 TON

crane called Big Blue

SILENT SUBMARINES

The stealthy 'black hole' subs that are undetectable in battle

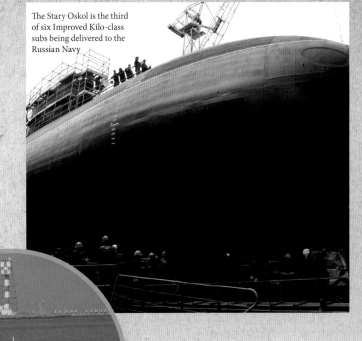

The Stary Oskol is the third of six Improved Kilo-class subs being delivered to the Russian Navy

They may be hard to miss when on dry land, but Improved Kilo-class submarines are able to travel unseen through the depths. These diesel-electric subs are considered to be the quietest in the world, leading NATO to nickname them 'black holes' due to their low noise and visibility. Despite weighing around 4,000 tons, the subs can reach speeds of 23 miles per hour, and can patrol for up to 45 days at a time.

Once they have snuck up on the enemy, eight infrared-guided surface-to-air missiles can then be fired at targets above the water, or computer-controlled torpedoes can be deployed beneath the waves. The submarine's array of sensors mean that it can detect enemy vessels at a range three to four times greater than it can be detected itself. This surveillance data can then be used by the onboard computer to calculate firing parameters and recommend maneuvers and weapon deployment. The six stealthy subs in this class were patrolling the Black Sea by the end of 2016.

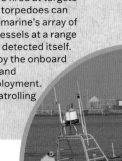

DRONE BOATS
THE UNMANNED VESSELS SAVING SAILORS FROM HIGH-RISK MISSIONS

With aerial drones already being used in military combat, it was only a matter of time before unmanned boats came onto the scene. The Royal Navy currently has a fleet of modified rigid inflatable boats (RIBs) in development that will be able to perform complex surveillance and reconnaissance missions, without putting sailors in harm's way. Using an arsenal of sensors, including a navigation radar, a 360-degree infrared camera array and a laser range finder, the vessels will be able to operate autonomously while avoiding collisions, and are expected to provide added protection for the Queen Elizabeth-class aircraft carriers once they enter service. The US Navy is also developing similar unmanned vessels that will be able to swarm and attack enemy targets, and the US defence agency DARPA even has plans for an 'Anti-Submarine Warfare Continuous Trail Unmanned Vehicle' that will be able to use artificial intelligence and sensors to hunt for enemy submarines.

LASER WEAPONS
THE SOUPED-UP LASER POINTER THAT CAN DESTROY COMBAT DRONES WITH DEADLY ACCURACY

The US Navy has turned science fiction into reality by developing a real-life laser gun that can blow up targets in an instant. Although they won't be using it to fight space aliens any time soon, the Laser Weapon System (LaWS) has been successfully tested at sea, proving that it is capable of blowing up moving targets on aerial drones and small boats. The weapon, which has been installed on board the USS Ponce, consists of six commercial welding lasers joined together, and can deliver 30 million times as much power as a hand-held laser pointer. It is operated using an Xbox-style controller and can be used to simply disable a target's sensors and instruments, or destroy it completely. As well as improved accuracy, another big advantage of LaWS is its cost, as the price of firing the laser is just 59 cents (39 pence) per shot, compared to the $2 million that is needed for a traditional missile.

Long range
The RIB drone can operate for 12 hours at a time, up to 25mi away from its parent ship

Complex missions
It can be used to patrol areas of interest, provide surveillance and reconnaissance, and protect larger ships in the fleet

Top speed
It can reach speeds of up to 44mi per hour on the water

Flexible control
It can operate autonomously on a pre-planned route or be remotely controlled by crew on land or the parent ship

Modified vessel
The drone is a modified version of the manned Pacific 24 RIB already in service on Type 23 Frigates and Type 45 Destroyers

LaWS is operational on board USS Ponce and can be used to defend against unmanned targets

A REVOLUTIONARY BATTLESHIP

How HMS Dreadnought launched a new era of naval power

When HMS Dreadnought entered service in 1906, it was the fastest and most powerful battleship in the world. Its propulsion, armament and fire control systems were so revolutionary that a new class of warship was soon named after it, with all battleships that came before simply labeled 'Pre-Dreadnought'. The new 'all big-gun' ship packed with advanced technology sent shockwaves around the world, reviving the naval arms race between Britain and Germany, and increasing tensions in the lead up to World War I. Other nations quickly began to copy the design, kick-starting a new era of ship development that changed naval warfare forever.

"THE NEW 'ALL BIG-GUN' SHIP PACKED WITH ADVANCED TECHNOLOGY SENT SHOCKWAVES AROUND THE WORLD"

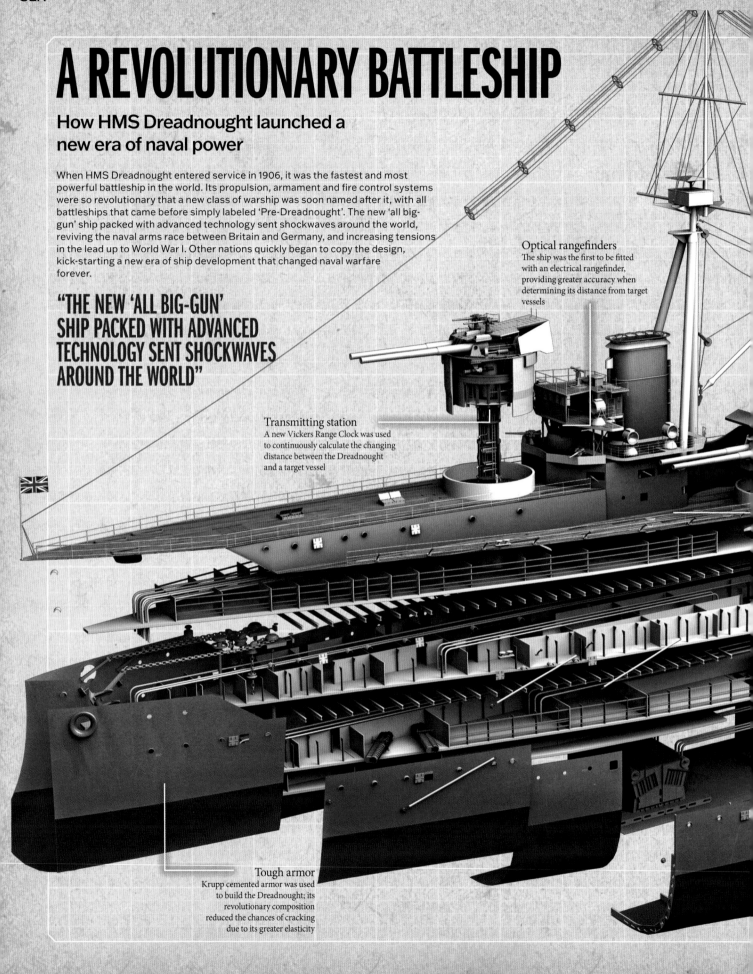

Optical rangefinders
The ship was the first to be fitted with an electrical rangefinder, providing greater accuracy when determining its distance from target vessels

Transmitting station
A new Vickers Range Clock was used to continuously calculate the changing distance between the Dreadnought and a target vessel

Tough armor
Krupp cemented armor was used to build the Dreadnought; its revolutionary composition reduced the chances of cracking due to its greater elasticity

Two of the Dreadnought's 12-inch Mark X guns ready to fire

FIREPOWER

As the first all big-gun battleship, HMS Dreadnought had astonishing firepower. Mounted on the top and sides of the ship were 12-pound guns that could defend against torpedo boats up to 5.3 miles away. For more distant targets, a further five 12-inch twin-gun turrets could be fired with a range of up to 14.3 miles, and as they all had identical ballistic characteristics, their firing ranges could be adjusted much more easily than guns of a different caliber. Plus, five 18-inch torpedo tubes could defend against attacking submarines.

THE STATISTICS...

HMS DREADNOUGHT

Length: 527ft	
Beam (width): 82ft	
Top speed: 24mph	
Crew: 700-810	
Range: 7,620mi	

Crew quarters
Officers and listed men were housed much closer to the bridge than usual to ensure they were closer to their action stations

A German Nassau-class battleship was built in response to the British HMS Dreadnought

Fuel supply
Nearly 3,000 tons of coal and over 1,000 tons of fuel oil could be carried on board, giving the ship a range of 7,620 miles

LIFE OF THE DREADNOUGHT

Despite being the dominant battleship of its era, HMS Dreadnought never actually managed to sink another battleship. The only major piece of action it saw came in 1915, when it was patrolling the North Sea during World War I. As a German SM U-29 submarine broke the surface ahead of it, a chase began. Eventually Dreadnought rammed into it and became the first battleship in history to sink a submarine.

While undergoing a refit in early 1916, it missed the now infamous Battle of Jutland, which saw the largest confrontation of battleships whose design the Dreadnought had inspired. HMS Dreadnought was decommissioned after the end of the First World War and eventually sold for scrap, but its iconic status as the most revolutionary battleship of its age lives on.

Fire doors
Passageways between the compartments below deck were removed and connecting doors were kept shut during combat to prevent the spread of possible fire or flooding

Turbine engines
Dreadnought was among the first battleships to use steam turbine engines, helping it reach the impressive speed of 24mph

Illustration by Alex Pang

HMS WARRIOR

The world's first iron-hulled, armor-plated warship is a marvel of engineering that symbolizes Victorian ingenuity and a forgotten naval arms race

Throughout the 19th century, Britain was the foremost naval power in the world. Since the Battle of Trafalgar in 1805, the Royal Navy achieved a supremacy that it would not lose for 150 years, but that did not mean it was without serious rivals. Although the British had defeated Napoleon Bonaparte in 1815, Bonapartism survived as a political force in France. In 1852 Napoleon's nephew became Emperor Napoleon III and started to reassert French military influence. This included an aggressive shipbuilding program, which culminated in the launch of La Gloire in 1859, the first ironclad (but wooden hulled) warship.

Determined to counter this threat, the British built an even bigger ship that was superior in every respect. The result was HMS Warrior, which was launched in 1860 and was the largest and fastest warship in the world. It was 60 percent bigger than La Gloire, heavily armored, armed to the teeth with 40 guns and manned by 705 crewmembers. Under full steam and sails, Warrior once achieved a top speed of 17.5 knots and was designed to be capable of an average of 15 knots.

To begin with there was no ship to match Warrior, which ironically resulted in it never seeing action – serving instead as an ironclad deterrent. Warrior saw service for over 20 years, mainly serving in the English Channel Squadron, but within five to seven years it became obsolete as its example kick-started the production of even bigger warships. Decommissioned in 1883, Warrior spent many years forgotten as a refueling depot but it was restored between 1979-85 to its former glory.

HMS Warrior is the first and only surviving example of the 'Black Battlefleet', the Royal Navy's 45 iron-hulled ships that were built between 1861-77

Above: Warrior had three sets of wheels on different decks. These wheels are on the gun deck and are known as 'battle wheels' as they were for use in action. It took eight men to operate them

"TO BEGIN WITH THERE WAS NO SHIP TO MATCH WARRIOR, WHICH IRONICALLY RESULTED IN IT NEVER SEEING ACTION – SERVING INSTEAD AS AN IRONCLAD DETERRENT"

HMS WARRIOR

MANUFACTURER **THAMES IRONWORKS & SHIPBUILDING COMPANY**
COMMISSIONED IN **1861**
LENGTH **418 FT**
BEAM **58 FT**
DRAUGHT **26 FT**
DISPLACEMENT **10,152 TONS**
SPEED **13 KNOTS UNDER SAIL, 15 KNOTS UNDER STEAM**
POWERPLANT **1 X JOHN PENN & SONS TWO-CYLINDER TRUNK STEAM ENGINE**
ARMAMENT **40 GUNS AND CANNON WITH ADDITIONAL SMALL ARMS**
CREW **705**

ARMAMENT

Warrior has one deck of guns, which includes 26 68-pounder cannon and ten rifled breech-loading guns. The varied ammunition consisted of smooth cannonballs, explosive shells, canister shots and even shells that could fire hot metal liquid. They were the largest and most modern guns of the period and could fire a broadside weight of over 1,360 kilograms. Warrior additionally had four 40-pounder guns on the upper deck and a variety of small arms including 350 Enfield rifles, 70 Colt Navy revolvers, cutlasses, axes and pikes.

Some of Warrior's Colt Navy revolvers are stored in an ornate weapons holder called a 'crocus'

Left: Warrior boasted two guns mounted on the upper deck. Mounted on sliding trucks, they allowed Warrior to engage an enemy in a chase

Warrior's single gun deck was a radical idea in a naval age of multiple decks, but its guns and cannon were the most powerful of their day

When all ten boilers were lit, temperatures could reach 50 degrees Celsius in the boiler rooms. Consequently, engineers, stokers and trimmers received a larger wage than seamen

"THE ENGINE TURNED THE PROPELLER SHAFT, WHICH EXTENDED OVER 100 FEET TO THE STERN WHERE THE PROPELLER BLADE WAS FITTED"

ENGINE, BOILERS AND... RAILWAY

There are ten boilers on board that are housed in two rooms, with each being capable of containing 18.7 tons of water. 937 tons of coal were used to heat them, which was housed in a bunker. Trimmers would shovel coal onto a railway system that ran between the bunker and boiler rooms and then pushed along trolleys to the relevant boiler. The steam produced powered the nearby twin-cylinder engine. The boiler and engine rooms were located in the middle of the ship so their combined weight did not affect the hull's trim. The engine turned the propeller shaft, which extended over 100 feet to the stern where the propeller blade was fitted.

HMS Warrior had a railway that ran the length of the boiler rooms along the underside of the boilers to deliver coal to the stokers

The ship's horizontal cylinder engine was economical with space and very efficient. The large cranks revolved at 56 rpm: approximately one revolution per second

Visitors to the captain's cabin would be hospitably received and guests included the British Prime Minister Lord Palmerston, members of the Royal Family and the kings of Greece and Egypt

Right: 650 men lived in close proximity to one another on the gun deck and 18 men would share a mess table for meals

QUARTERS

The quality of accommodation aboard Warrior depended on rank. Out of a crew of 705, 650 lived on the gun deck, with 18 men per mess table. These men slept in hammocks and lived in close to the guns. There was more privacy for officers who slept in individual cabins with bunks. The chief engineer, captain of Marines and four paymasters also had cabins.

Warrior's pre-eminence in the Royal Navy gave its captain an exalted status and he was known as 'Second only unto God'. Consequently, his cabin was large enough to entertain heads of state and government for diplomatic occasions with the best plate, food and furniture available. Legend has it that the only exalted dignitary who didn't visit Warrior was Queen Victoria herself.

HMS Warrior is berthed in the Portsmouth Historic Dockyard complex and is open to the public. For more details visit www.hmswarrior.org

HMS WARRIOR
1860

"WARRIOR WAS A REVOLUTIONARY SHIP IN TERMS OF STRUCTURE, ARMORED WITH 4.5IN OF WROUGHT IRON, 18.1IN OF TEAK AND THEN 0.9IN OF THE SHIP'S IRON HULL"

Above: Engineers and stokers wore white uniforms to be visible while shoveling coal in dark conditions. Their clothes were regularly cleaned in these manual washing machines

A cross section of Warrior's bulkhead armor. From left to right is the iron hull, teak and armor plating

NAVAL INNOVATIONS

Warrior was a revolutionary ship in terms of structure and crew welfare. It is armored with 4.5 inches of wrought iron, backed by 18.1 inches of teak and then 0.9 inches of the ship's actual iron hull.

This metal cocoon encompassed some enlightened naval practices. The crew were volunteers who were guaranteed regular pay, pensions and vocational courses. They had easy access to fresh water from condensers, tightly controlled rum rations and an improved diet. The importance of personal hygiene was also recognized, so Warrior features a complex of bathrooms and laundry facilities. It was compulsory to bathe regularly and there were steam-injected hand-cranked washing machines and an innovative laundry drying room, which was coal-fired.

HMS
BELFAST

WORDS **TOM GARNER** WITH THANKS TO **MICHAEL SMITH** & **RACHAEL CAMPBELL**

This powerful reminder of Britain's naval might in the early 20th century helped sink the Scharnhorst and led the Allied naval bombardment on D-Day

Located in the heart of central London HMS Belfast is a unique naval survivor from World War II and the Korean War

Image © Imperial War Museum

HMS Belfast is one of the finest surviving examples of a World War II battleship in existence and has an impressive history. It was launched on Saint Patrick's Day in 1938 by the wife of then-Prime Minister Neville Chamberlain, and was commissioned into the Royal Navy on 5 August 1939, almost exactly in time for the war. Belfast was the largest cruiser in the fleet, and was immediately called into service patrolling northern waters. However, in November 1939, Belfast struck a mine in the Firth of Forth and the extensive damage took two and a half years to repair.

On rejoining the fleet in 1942, Belfast was newly equipped with advanced radar systems and played a crucial role in protecting Arctic convoys, most notably at the Battle of North Cape where it participated in the sinking of the German battleship Scharnhorst. In 1944, Belfast would have been the ship that transported Winston Churchill to the D-Day landings but King George VI prevented him from going. Belfast was among the first ships to open fire on 6 June and spent 33 days at Normandy, expending more than 5,000 shells.

After the end of the war, Belfast played an active role in Korea from 1950-52, working with other naval forces to support United Nations troops and firing more than 8,000 shells during the entire conflict. The ship was later modernized for nuclear warfare before being decommissioned in 1963. Since 1971, Belfast has been a museum ship and is permanently moored in London on the River Thames near Tower Bridge.

"IN 1944, BELFAST WOULD HAVE BEEN THE SHIP THAT TRANSPORTED WINSTON CHURCHILL TO THE D-DAY LANDINGS BUT KING GEORGE VI PREVENTED HIM FROM GOING"

HMS BELFAST

MANUFACTURER	HARLAND AND WOLFF SHIPYARD
COMMISSIONED	5 AUGUST 1939
LENGTH	613.6 FEET
BEAM	69 FEET
DRAUGHT	19.9 FEET
DISPLACEMENT	11,175 TONS
SPEED	32 KNOTS (37 MPH)
POWERPLANT	4 X OIL-FIRED, THREE-DRUM STEAM BOILERS POWERING FOUR PARSONS SINGLE REDUCTION GEARED STEAM TURBINES
ARMAMENT	12 X 152MM MK XXIII GUNS, 16 X 40 MM TWO-POUNDER ANTI-AIRCRAFT CANNONS, 8 X 13MM ANTI-AIRCRAFT CANNONS
AIR ARM	2 X SUPERMARINE WALRUS RECON BIPLANES
CREW	850

HMS Belfast bombarding German positions in Normandy, June 1944. The ship was one of the first Allied vessels to fire on D-Day at 5.27am

BOILER ROOM AND ENGINES

Belfast's stokers likened stepping into the boiler room to stepping into hell: the temperature ranged between 86-104 degrees Fahrenheit. The complex machinery generated superheated steam at about 752 degrees Fahrenheit to help power the engines. There are four boilers and fuel tanks carrying 2,425 tons of oil, and Belfast's four turbine engines rely on unit-propulsion. Each engine has four turbines for pressure, cruising and reversing, and they were operated by university-educated artificers. When all four engines were working together, the ship would get through two to three tonnes of oil per hour but this would increase to 28.6 to 31.9 tons per hour at the full speed of 32 knots.

Right: During the 1950s modernization refit, a panel was installed so that the boilers could be manned from the engine room, thus giving the artificers more control

Below: The working temperatures in the vast labyrinths of the boiler rooms could be extreme, between 30-40 degrees Celsius. Stokers were constantly supplied with lemonade and salt tablets to prevent dehydration

Left: The engine order telegraph was used to communicate commands between the bridge and engine room

The forward triple turrets of HMS Belfast. Combined with the men in the shell and cordite rooms below, it could take up to 50 men to control one turret

"LOADING AND FIRING ONE GUN CAN TAKE LESS THAN TEN SECONDS AND THE RATE OF FIREPOWER IS EIGHT ROUNDS PER MINUTE"

Each shell weighed 110 pounds, which the admiralty said was the largest that a man could lift by hand

Nine men worked in the shell room, and in heavy action could get 30 rounds of ammunition up to the guns per minute

ARMAMENT

Belfast has multiple triple gun turrets with each one containing a crew of 27. There would be seven men around the breaches, a turret captain, observer, sight-setter, gun trainer, ordnance suppliers and mechanics. The middle barrel in each turret would be set slightly behind the other barrels so that shells wouldn't interfere with each other in flight. Loading and firing one gun could take less than ten seconds and the rate of firepower is eight rounds per-minute. The guns were supplied from shell rooms directly below the turrets. Each room held 600 rounds of ammunition, equating to 2,400 rounds for the whole ship and 200 rounds per gun.

Left: HMS Belfast fires a salvo against enemy troop concentrations on the west coast of Korea in March 1951. The Korean War was the last time Belfast fired its guns on active service

The enclosed bridge was designed to protect the captain in an age of nuclear warfare. It also contains the ship's strikingly mounted main compass (center)

Below: By the 1950s, radar was replacing eyes as the main naval sighting device, which enabled the bridge to be enclosed with a reduced viewing platform

BRIDGE

Before the refit of 1956-59, Belfast's bridge was open air, but the captain was moved inside with the advent of nuclear warfare. This is a bridge designed for the Cold War and is positioned at the highest possible level. It also doubles as the main compass platform. Previously, the captain needed a 360-degree view of the surrounding area, but by the 1950s, radar was doing most of the work, enabling the windows to only face forward, port and starboard. There is also no helm as it is stationed in the bottom of the hull. This was so the ship could keep steering if it came under attack.

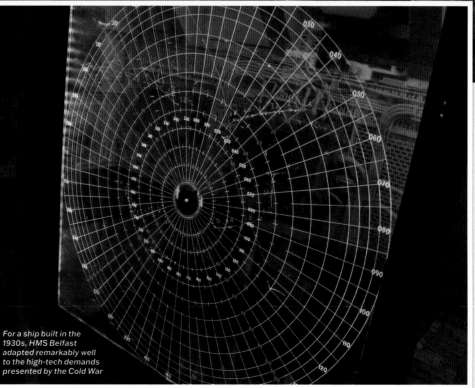

For a ship built in the 1930s, HMS Belfast adapted remarkably well to the high-tech demands presented by the Cold War

INFORMATION AND TRANSMITTING STATIONS

After 1959, Belfast was a recognizably modern warship. The captain and his main officers would be located in the action information office to act on targets picked up by radar and the direction control tower. The captain could make an informed decision in one spot based on data from readers, chart tables and repeaters. In the transmitting station, there is a mechanical computer from World War II that predates the refit. Exclusively operated by Marines, the computer made calculations about air pressure, wind speed, drift and targets in order to aim and elevate Belfast's guns at precise angles.

During the Cold War, the captain and his senior officers worked in this command center where compiled information enabled them to make quick decisions

Belfast contains a World War II computer (center) that calculated the firing angles for the guns. Remarkably, the technology for these machines actually dates back to World War I

Left: Belfast was equipped with two Supermarine Walrus amphibious biplanes that were used to attack submarines. They were launched by catapult and had hangars to store them when not in use

"THERE IS NO HELM ON THE BRIDGE OF HMS BELFAST AS IT IS STATIONED IN THE BOTTOM OF THE HULL. THIS WAS SO THE SHIP COULD KEEP STEERING IF IT CAME UNDER ATTACK"

HMS MEDUSA

In June 1944, HMS Medusa served as the lead navigation ship on D-Day, guiding Allied crafts through enemy minefields

During the course of WWII, over 480 Harbor Defence Motor Launches (HDMLs) were built to defend the United Kingdom's coasts against the German submarine threat. In the early years of the war there was a real fear U-boats could encircle the country and cut off its vital ports and harbors, so these small vessels were intended to build a screen of defence, identifying and sinking any enemy boats. When this threat didn't materialize, the HDMLs were put to work in a whole range of other tasks, such as defending convoys, inserting agents into enemy territory and supporting attacks on islands.

The vessels truly came into their own during Operation Neptune, when they guided Allied craft through the deadly enemy minefields

The HMS Medusa, commission in 1943 and built in Poole, UK, served allied ships during the war, guiding them through enemy waters

of the English Channel on D-Day. In the lead up to the assault, minesweepers carved two channels towards Omaha beach, where American troops would soon be facing some of the toughest resistance of the landings. Vessels ML 1383 and 1387 were positioned as beacons to these channels and would remain for over 30 hours, guiding the Allied craft packed with men and equipment on their way to the beaches of Normandy.

Designed to be small, silent, agile and incredibly flexible, HDMLs weren't intended for longevity. Of the original 480 or so craft, only one remains operational today: ML 1387, now called HMS Medusa. Built in Poole, UK, in 1943, the Medusa took part in Exercise Fabius in May 1944, which was a practice operation for D-Day, before providing crucial support of the landings themselves.

Left: The crew of HMS Medusa, HDML 1397, including Commanding Officer SLt Arthur Maurice Liddiard RNVR

Below: At its current moorings in Gosport, UK

ML1387

ML 1387 'HMS MEDUSA'

COMMISSIONED: 29 DECEMBER 1943
CREW: 12
LENGTH: 72 FEET
ORIGIN: DORSET, UK
TOP SPEED: 12 KNOTS
ENGINE: TWIN DIESEL GARDNER 8L3S
WEIGHT: 54 TONS (WATER DISPLACEMENT)

"HDMLS WERE PUT TO WORK DEFENDING CONVOYS, INSERTING AGENTS INTO ENEMY TERRITORY AND SUPPORTING ATTACKS"

The Chart Room aboard the HMS Medusa. This was where Sub Lt Maurice Liddiard would have outlined the ship's involvement in D-Day

P3516

OERLIKON 20MM AUTOMATIC CANNON

Each of the two deck-mounted cannons were manned by one gunner strapped in by a harness. This helped the gunner to easily maneuver the weapon almost 360 degrees, as well as upward to almost a fully vertical angle. A safety feature was built into the mechanism of the mount to prevent the weapon rotating a full 360 degrees, as gunners were prone to accidentally damaging their own vessel as they turned and followed their target. The guns carried 60-round magazines, and were capable of delivering 480 rounds per minute. This meant even a brief squeeze of the trigger for mere seconds could expel an entire magazine into the enemy. Bursts of fire like this were ideal against diving Stuka bombers and other aircraft.

The maneuverability of the 20mm gun made it perfect for leveling fire at both aircraft and targets on the surface

Two nearby lockers each contained four extra magazines for reloading the gun

Medusa currently has only one 20mm gun, put together from donations and chance findings at scrap yards

TWIN VICKERS 'K' MACHINE GUNS

Two twin Vickers machine guns could be mounted on the vessel, one each on the port and starboard sides. These gas-operated guns were each capable of between 900 and 1,200 rounds per minute and were originally developed for the RAF. They were ideal for dealing with enemy aircraft, as well as providing supporting fire.

THE BRIDGE

From here the commanding officer could raise an action-stations alarm, as well as communicate to the engineer and the radio operator below deck. The Engine Order Telegraph (EOT) would deliver orders to the engineer, with one lever for each engine. A bell ringing in the engine room alerted the engineer, who would then adjust the revs of each engine to correspond to the order from the EOT at his end. Just like EOTs used on much larger vessels, the orders included Full Ahead, Stop and Slow, but because it took a small amount of time to adjust each engine, slowing or accelerating the vessel would not have happened instantly.

The EOT system was typical of much larger vessels, but was included on HDMLs as standard

ELECTRONIC WARFARE ON D-DAY

MEDUSA WAS EQUIPPED WITH SOME OF THE MOST CUTTING-EDGE TECHNOLOGY, ALL MANNED BELOW DECK BY A LONE OPERATOR

GEE NAVIGATION SYSTEM

Designed for the RAF to improve the accuracy of its bombers, this system was accurate to within a quarter of a mile. Three stations on the shore would send out simultaneous pulses, each of which would be received by the Gee, then the timings between each pulse would determine the location of the vessel. Because it was feared that the Germans would be able to block the signal of the Gee, new transmitters and receiver modules were developed just for D-Day.

DECCA SYSTEM (QM)

Developed in Canada and tested at the Firth of Forth, where it was less-likely to be picked up by the Germans, this system was kept highly secret prior to D-Day to prevent it being jammed. The system was integral to the planning of Operation Neptune, even to the point that ship positions, movements and routes were planned with the Decca signal in mind. Only 20 of these units were used on the most-essential vessels during D-Day and Medusa was only one of two HDMLs to be fitted with one.

TYPE 291 RADAR

This standard-issue radar was adapted from a system used on Sunderland flying boats. Much less-sophisticated than modern-day PPI (Plan Position Indicator) displays, the Type 291 could simply guess how far away a target was. It was capable of identifying a destroyer at around six miles away. An IFF system (Indicate Friend Foe) would also indicate where allied or unidentified objects were in the area.

THE ENGINE ROOM

HDMLs were fitted with two diesel engines and one generator to charge the electricity. There would be an engineer manning the engine room at all times, on alternating shifts of 12 hours. Cruising at around 600 revs per minute, the vessel would consume an average of seven gallons of fuel per hour between all three engines. With room to store 1,550 gallons of fuel on board, the vessel could stay at sea for over 2,000 nautical miles. It was the job of the engineer to ensure that fuel was consumed equally between tanks on both the port and starboard sides of the boat, so that the craft remained level and balanced, rather than lopsided.

Below: In the event a depth charge was dropped to attack a submarine, the engineer could boost each engine's revs to 900 per minute so the vessel could escape the blast!

Above: The two engines could produce less than 300 horsepower between them – they were built for endurance, not power

Below: Engines were regularly swapped out of older and into newer craft by the Admiralty and weren't originally designed to last more than five years

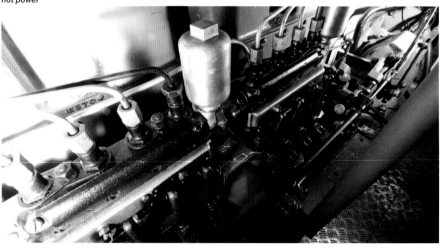

SUBMARINE DETECTION

The original purpose of HDMLs was to seek out and destroy submarines. A large metal dome on the underside of the vessel would send out sonar pings, which would then return back any objects within range. The size and direction of a submarine would be displayed on the automatic graph, and the crew would easily be able to maneuver the vessel to pursue it.

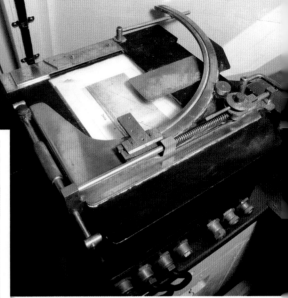

This box (left) contained a detonator that was to be used by the commanding officer to destroy all the classified equipment on the vessel, if it were at risk of being captured by the enemy

THE WARDROOM

The skipper and first officer occupied this room near the aft of the vessel. Though it was nearly the exact size of the galley area, which housed six of the crew, the two officers occupied this space in relative comfort, complete with an alcohol cabinet, furnishings and the vessel's safe. This safe contained the crew's pay, the captain's orders, side arms, a flare gun and any other sensitive documents. A bell system connected to the galley was also in place, for the officers to call for their meals or other attention from the crew. It was here that refugees hid when they were aboard the vessel.

THE MEDUSA TRUST
WWW.HMSMEDUSA.ORG.UK

Set up in 2003, the Medusa Trust worked tirelessly to raise funds for the refit of the vessel, which was in need of drastic restoration work. "In order to do the sort of fundraising we needed to do, she needed to be part of a charitable trust," says Medusa's current skipper and Chairman of the Trust Alan Watson. "The whole purpose of the Trust was to restore, operate and maintain this vessel, but it has broadened slightly. As well as this vessel we're also guardians of the history of all the HDMLs... We are the last crew of the last HDML now, which is a bit special." Along with coxswain and historian of the Medusa, Brian Holmes, the Trust continues to piece together the history of these vessels and the stories of their crew for future generations.

SUBMARINES OF THE WORLD

Discover the globe's best-known subs and their infamous encounters

❶ RECON AT MIDWAY
PACIFIC OCEAN 4 JUNE 1942

US submarines prove to be key in ascertaining the strength and location of the Japanese fleet converging on Midway. In the ensuing battle, the US claims a decisive Pacific victory and the Imperial fleet is damaged beyond repair.

Alligator
Produced: 1862
Speciality: Protecting wooden ships from Confederate ironclads
Location: Philadelphia, USA

HL Hunley
Produced: 1863
Speciality: Hunting Union warships
Location: Alabama, USA

❷ UNDER THE POLE
THE NORTH POLE 3 AUGUST 1958

USS Nautilus, the world's first nuclear-powered submarine, makes history by reaching the North Pole and crossing it submerged, having set off from the United States some two months prior.

USS Nautilus enters New York Harbor in January 1956

Vetehinen-class
Produced: 1930
Speciality: Coastal mine-laying
Location: Finland

Whiskey-class
Produced: 1949
Speciality: Coastal patrol
Location: Russia

Kalev-class
Produced: 1935
Speciality: Laying mines
Location: Estonia

Rota-ßclass
Produced: 1918
Speciality: Torpedo warfare
Location: Denmark

Daphné-class
Produced: 1958
Speciality: Patrol and achieving greater depths
Location: Cherbourg, France

Katsonis-class
Produced: 1925
Speciality: Offensive maneuvers
Location: Greece

Type-209
Produced: 1971
Speciality: Widely used deterrent
Location: Turkey

Soviet K-class
Produced: 1936
Speciality: Long-range search and destroy
Location: Leningrad, Soviet Union

Tikuna
Produced: 1996
Speciality: Attack submarine
Location: Brazil

Scorpéne-class
Produced: 1999
Speciality: Offensive operations
Location: Chile

❸ THE FALKLANDS WAR
FALKLAND ISLANDS 30 APRIL 1982

The United Kingdom imposes a Total Exclusion Zone that surrounds the Falkland Islands, encompassing an area of 200 nautical miles. Any ships that enter this zone are fair game for British submarines.

❹ KURSK DISASTER
NEAR MURMANSK, RUSSIA
12 AUGUST 2000

Oscar-class Russian sub Kursk is destroyed following a number of on-board torpedo explosions. The entirety of the boat's crew is killed, either by the initial explosions or from asphyxiation as fires break out in the aftermath.

The Kursk disaster claimed the lives of 118 Russian sailors, the full crew including five officers and two engineers

HMS Vanguard returns to HM Naval Base Clyde following CASD patrol in 2010

❺ NUCLEAR TEST
FASLANE, SCOTLAND
26 MAY 1994

HMS Vanguard initiates the first test launch of a British nuclear Trident missile. Vanguard went on to embark on the first patrol that year in what is now the UK's ongoing strategy of continuous at-sea deterrence (CASD).

❶

❻ ATLANTIC BATTLE
JUST SOUTH-EAST OF BEAUFORT INLET, NORTH CAROLINA, USA
9 MAY 1942

German submarine U-352 is bested by patrol boat USCGC Icarus, under the command of the US Coast Guard. She is destroyed with depth charges, and her crew is taken prisoner by the US Navy.

❼ UNDERWATER COLLISION
BAY OF BISCAY
4 FEBRUARY 2009

HMS Vanguard and French submarine Le Triomphant collide with each other in the Bay of Biscay, in what is a rather embarrassing incident for both the British and French Ministries of Defence. Both are nuclear subs, yet fortunately only sustain light damage.

❽ LUSITANIA SUNK
SOUTHERN COAST OF IRELAND
7 MAY 1915

German U-boat U-20 fires a torpedo at HMS Lusitania, a passenger liner bound for Britain from New York. She sinks in only 18 minutes. A total of 1,195 passengers and crew are thought to have drowned.

Type AM
Produced: 1943
Speciality: Command boats carrying sea-planes
Location: Japan

Ghadir-class
Produced: 2006
Speciality: Recon and direct attack
Location: Tehran, Iran

Collins-class
Produced: 1990
Speciality: Attack sub
Location: Australia

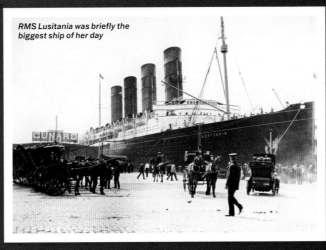

RMS Lusitania was briefly the biggest ship of her day

Corbis

HEAD TO HEAD

If the Cold War had ever heated up, there was plenty of firepower on offer. Here are two opposing nuclear submarines that served in these years of military tension

K-43
SOVIET NAVY, RUSSIAN NAVY

MISSILES

The K-43 was the first Soviet submarine with submerged launch SS-N-7 anti-ship missiles (eight of them, in fact) so it didn't have to make risky surfaces.

TORPEDOES

Either 12 SS-N-15 anti-submarine missiles or 12 torpedoes were fitted to the K-43, giving it a formidable underwater arsenal.

SPEED

Using its single five-blade propeller, the K-43 could reach a speed of 16 knots when surfaced and 23 knots when underwater.

POWER TYPE

A first-generation VM-5 nuclear reactor was used to propel the ship and powered the impressive 20,000shp steam turbine.

TECHNOLOGY

This advanced submarine contained the all-new Snoop Tray surface-search radar, which helped seek out targets for missile strikes.

TOTAL

THE PROJECT 670 CHARLIE CLASS

The K-43 was one of 17 submarines in the USSR's nuclear-powered Project 670 Charlie class. The class was split into two, with the K-43 forming the first group of subs. The first batches of Soviet submarines were diesel-electric powered and based on captured German models, but Charlie was part of the new nuclear unit launched in 1967. The class' main role in the Soviet Navy was surprise attacks on aircraft carriers. The model survived the fall of the Soviet Union and was retired in 1994. It was succeeded by the Papa class of submarine, which boasted a titanium hull and a higher top speed.

The K-43 operated in the Soviet Navy until 1988 when it was sold to the Indian Navy

"THE CLASS'S MAIN ROLE IN THE SOVIET NAVY WAS SURPRISE ATTACKS ON AIRCRAFT CARRIERS"

Trident missiles were first introduced in 1979 and are still used by both the US and UK

This submarine was named after Kazimierz Puɫaski (1745–1779), a Polish General who fought for the US in the American War of Independence

USS CASIMIR PULASKI

MISSILES

The submarine was armed with either 16 Polaris or Poseidon ballistic missiles that made use of the first ever satellite navigation system, TRANSIT.

TORPEDOES

Four MK-45 nuclear torpedoes were held onboard. An airlock was used to adjust the projectile to the change in atmospheric pressure when launched into the sea.

SPEED

The Casimir Pulaski could easily race to speeds of over 20 knots, giving it a slight pace advantage over its Soviet rivals from the era.

POWER TYPE

Two steam turbines were turned by a S5W nuclear core, a new type of propulsion system that replaced the S1W in 1971.

TECHNOLOGY

Noise-dampening technology was used to make the submarine as undetectable as possible and the vessel contained a Trident missile targeting system.

TOTAL

"TO ACCOMMODATE THE ADVANCED MISSILES, THE SUBMARINES WERE FITTED WITH THE BEST GUIDANCE AND NAVIGATION SYSTEMS MONEY COULD BUY"

ANATOMY OF A...
TYPE VII U-BOAT

The most prolific military submersible ever built, German U-boats presented a major threat to Allied shipping in the Atlantic and elsewhere

ALL-SEEING EYE
Another famous feature of both historical and contemporary submarine design, the periscope allows a submarine crew to observe goings-on both in the water and on the surface. By utilizing mirrors, the periscope enabled U-boat crews to observe targets on the surface of the water without revealing the submarine's location

CONNING TOWER
The conning tower was a common feature of submarines, but was and is found on many sea vessels. Although not actually the U-boat's command center, despite its prominent placement, it was the area in which periscopes were operated in order to conduct reconnaissance and direct torpedo attacks

DECK GUN
The Type VII came complete with an 88mm cannon located just in front of the conning tower. Quite obviously this could only be used while the submarine was surfaced, but it presented an effective form of secondary defence

TORPEDO ARSENAL
Key to any submarine in wartime, the Type VII carried a number of torpedoes on board, with its payload more than enough to cause considerable trouble for enemy submersibles and surface ships. The G7e torpedo was electric-propelled, and was the standard-issue torpedo of the war

TYPE VII U-BOAT

YEARS IN USE: **1936-1970**
COUNTRY OF ORIGIN: **GERMANY**
ENGINE SIZE: **6-CYLINDER 4-STROKE X2**
WATER DISPLACEMENT: **UP TO 1,080 TONS**
MAXIMUM DEPTH: **722 FEET**
TOP SPEED: **8 KNOTS (SUBMERGED)**
WEAPONS: **TORPEDOES, MINES AND DECK GUNS**
CREW: **UP TO 60, INCLUDING 4 OFFICERS**

BALLAST TANKS
Ballast tanks served an extremely important purpose – they enabled the submarine to ascend and descend vertically. It's simple science, and an elegant solution – tanks inside the hull of the U-boat took on water to reduce buoyancy and enable the vessel to sink down out of sight

The U-boat U-36 – a prime example of the German Type VIIA model submarine

ANTI-AIRCRAFT GUNS

If a Type VII were ever forced to return to the surface, it had some countermeasures on hand for any Allied aircraft that fancied taking a pop. This model would have been fitted with a 20mm flak cannon with a high rate of fire – more than enough to take down an Allied bird

CREW QUARTERS

Life on a submarine was and still is difficult to adjust to. The crew quarters on a German U-boat were much like those found on other submarines of the Second World War – modest but functional. There were bunks, a lavatory and a small mess

ENGINE ROOM

The meat and bones of the vessel, the Type VII U-boat's engine room housed its two six-cylinder, four-stroke diesel engines. Also on board were electric engines powered by two large batteries that enabled the boat to move while it was submerged. The diesel engines acted as dynamos, recharging the electric motors while the submarine was surfaced

PROPELLERS AND RUDDER

On the surface, these Type VIIs operated in much the same way as any other vessel. As expected, the propellers were key for driving the submersible forwards at a reasonable rate, while the rudder enabled left and right turns – this was very important when it came to navigating around mines and other dangerous obstacles

SINGLE HULL

Like most antiquated submarine designs, the Type VII U-boat employed a single hull, but it was also reinforced with sturdy rib-like bands of steel to further fortify its outer shell. This was mostly to protect the craft against water pressure at significant depths

DK Images

HMS ALLIANCE

Take a tour of the mechanics, weapons and operating systems of Britain's last surviving Second World War submarine

A veteran submarine hunter from the Cold War, HMS Alliance is a diesel-electric submarine and the tenth constructed from the Amphion class of the Royal Navy. The 16 in its class were ordered to be constructed in 1943 when Imperial Japan was becoming a danger to the Allies in the Pacific theater of war. However, by V-J Day none of the submarines had been commissioned in time to see battle and were instead thrust into the Cold War.

Alliance was designed for long-distance patrolling at a range of around 10,000 miles with up to 30 days underwater. The submarine used a technique learnt from the Germans called 'snorkeling' or 'snorting', which allowed the vessel to travel long distances with a steady supply of fresh air. Alliance went under a huge overhaul in 1958 to get it up to speed with the tough seas of the Cold War. With the new additions it became a key part of the Royal Navy despite running aground in 1968

and a fire in 1971 that killed one crewmember and injured 14.

The submarine slipped into retirement in 1973 as the Oberon and Porpoise classes of submarine took over. It was then used as training boat until 1981, when it became a memorial to the 4,334 submariners who lost their lives in both World Wars and the 739 who have been killed in peacetime disasters. It is now the centerpiece of the Royal Navy Submarine Museum in Gosport, Hampshire.

Left *HMS Alliance clocked up thousands of miles as it monitored submarines from the Red Fleet during the Cold War*

HMS ALLIANCE

TYPE: A-CLASS FIGHTING VESSEL
COMMISSIONED: 14 MAY 1947
ORIGIN: UK
LENGTH: 281FT
ENGINE: TWIN DIESEL-ELECTRIC
CREW: 68 (FIVE OFFICERS, 63 RATINGS)
TOP SPEED: 18.5 KNOTS (SURFACED) 8 KNOTS (SUBMERGED)
PRIMARY WEAPON: 12 MARK VIII TORPEX TORPEDOES
SECONDARY WEAPONS: 4IN GUN, 20MM AA GUN, 3 .303 MACHINE GUNS, 26 MINES

"ALLIANCE WAS DESIGNED FOR LONG-DISTANCE PATROLLING AT A RANGE OF AROUND 10,000 MILES WITH UP TO 30 DAYS UNDERWATER"

Left: *With its all-welded hull, Alliance made submarines stronger and quicker off the production line*

Below: *Alliance as it looks today. The museum was given £7 million in 2013 to stop it rusting away*

TORPEDOES

The weapon systems of Alliance were vital, despite the fact that the Cold War never reached open hostilities. The vessel could carry up to 12 torpedoes at a time, which would be fired in a triple salvo at enemy submarines and ships.

The weapons of choice for the Alliance were two-ton Mark VIII torpedoes with a 730lb explosive torpex head. These would be fired just below the surface at the side of a ship for maximum damage. The Mark VIII would later be phased out by the Tigerfish Torpedo, which boasted a magnetic proximity fuse that would explode when in the locality of the target.

Four torpedo tubes were placed at the front with a further two at the rear if the submarine was being pursued

CONTROL ROOM

The control room is the central hub of HMS Alliance. The submarine would be steadied by two leading seamen who would keep the vessel level and at the right depth while a helmsman steered. They would be joined by an officer who would be in charge of releasing and flooding the lower decks with water for balance and a navigation officer and his assistant, who would plot the course. Naturally, the captain of the vessel would most often be present in the control room.

The Alliance has two periscopes: the 'search' was used for everyday use while the 'attack' periscope was used when action stations was called. The room would commonly be manned by eight crewmen but this could rise to 25 in action stations.

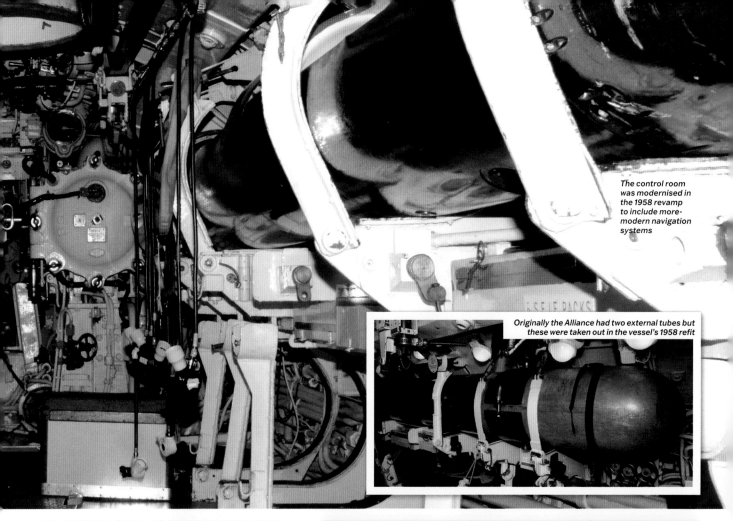

The control room was modernised in the 1958 revamp to include more-modern navigation systems

Originally the Alliance had two external tubes but these were taken out in the vessel's 1958 refit

"THE WEAPONS OF CHOICE FOR THE ALLIANCE WERE TWO-TON MARK VIII TORPEDOES WITH A 730LB EXPLOSIVE"

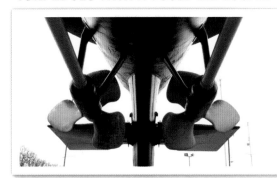

PROPELLERS

Thanks to its diesel-electric system, the HMS Alliance was capable of 18.5 knots on the surface and eight knots when submerged. Sluggish when compared with the ships of the era, this was equal to the majority of submarines at least until the nuclear era led by the launch of USS Nautilus.

Although imposing, the propellers were remarkably quiet and the Alliance was an extremely discreet ship, which helped it no end when tracking Soviet subs across the oceans. The boat's direction was controlled from the stern by fore planes, which adjusted depth, and after planes that controlled the angle of the submarine.

THE OTHER AMPHION-CLASS SUBS
WHAT HAPPENED TO ALLIANCE'S SISTER SUBMARINES?

HMS ALDERNEY (P416)

Like the Alliance, Alderney underwent an expensive refit in 1958 to get it up to scratch. The submarine was part of various Royal Navy submarine squadrons and was primarily used in training exercises with the Royal Canadian Navy and Air Force. It was decommissioned in 1966 and eventually scrapped in 1970.

HMS AFFRAY

The last Royal Navy submarine lost at sea, HMS Affray was involved in a training exercise that went horribly wrong in April 1951. The Submarine sunk during the operation in the English Channel after supposed system defects or possible battery explosion. All 75 of the crew perished in the disaster.

HMS ARTFUL

The Artful was put on loan to the Royal Canadian Navy as a training submarine in 1951 but returned to the reserve and the 5th Submarine Squadron in 1954. From then on it participated in Home Fleet Squadron Tours until its scrapping in 1972.

ENGINE ROOM

The engine room was by far and away the nosiest, hottest and dirtiest place on the submarine. The twin diesel-electric engines dominated the room, which was hot and humid at nearly all times. Seasickness was common in this room and the pointed stern of the submarine made the area move in a figure of eight when advancing through the sea.

The lives of the engineers on board weren't safe either – as space is lacking on a submarine, open valves and electrical circuits were everywhere. Some of these open blades could have up to 440 volts of direct current running through them. With the advent of nuclear subs, the safety aspects of their engine rooms were forced to become a priority, for obvious reasons.

The engine room shook so much, many submariners strapped buckets to themselves for when seasickness struck!

THE 1958 REFIT

HMS Alliance was built for the war in the Pacific and Far East operations, so when the Second World War ended and the Cold War escalated, some of its features became obsolete. The 20mm anti-aircraft gun was deemed surplus to requirements, as rival submarines became the enemy rather than ships and aircraft. The 1958 refit concentrated on making the Alliance much more streamlined so it was even quieter than it had been and therefore more difficult for sonar to detect. As nuclear submarines began to take over, HMS Alliance didn't find itself becoming obsolete. Instead it occupied a much more niche role of obtaining information and undertaking reconnaissance missions.

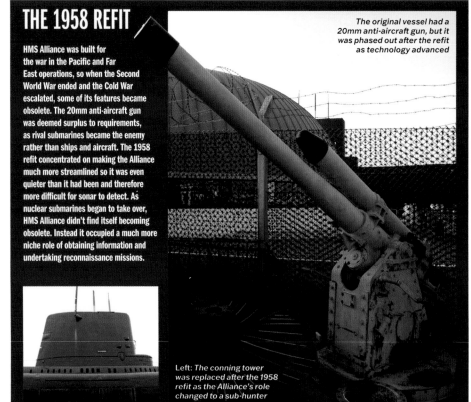

The original vessel had a 20mm anti-aircraft gun, but it was phased out after the refit as technology advanced

Left: The conning tower was replaced after the 1958 refit as the Alliance's role changed to a sub-hunter

"THE TWIN DIESEL-ELECTRIC ENGINES DOMINATED THE ROOM, WHICH WAS HOT AND HUMID AT NEARLY ALL TIMES"

As part of the recent restoration project, the stern has been reconstructed following corrosion damage

ROYAL NAVY SUBMARINE MUSEUM

The Royal Navy Submarine Museum has been at its current location in Gosport, Hampshire, since 1978. HMS Alliance was donated to the museum in the same year as its principal exhibit. The museum attracts 50,000 visitors a year and doubles up as a memorial to all British submariners who have given their lives in service. Its continuing mission is to tell the story of the Royal Navy Submarine Service.

Visit www.submarine-museum.co.uk for opening hours and admission information.

LIFE ABOARD A SUBMARINE

JJ MOLLOY SERVED AS A WEAPONS ENGINEER ON HMS WALRUS, HMS OPPORTUNE AND HMS SEALION DURING THE COLD WAR

WHY DID YOU CHOOSE TO JOIN THE NAVY AND BECOME A SUBMARINER?

I joined the navy thinking I would go onto aircraft carriers and have a good life sunning myself in warm climates. I finished my training but I was drafted onto submarines instead.

WHAT'S IT LIKE TO BE OUT AT SEA AND UNDER THE WAVES ON WHAT ARE OFTEN LONG OPERATIONS?

It's a very peaceful existence. The submarines are designed to be quiet and the crew is quiet. You get up, do your job and go back to bed. It's all about routine. You don't really notice the space after a while because you're so used to it. Everyone knows where they've got to be and what they've got to do, so you don't bump into people. Claustrophobia has never been a problem.

WHAT WERE YOUR DAY-TO-DAY DUTIES LIKE WHEN YOU WERE ON BOARD THE SUBMARINE?

Although I was a weapons engineer, the duties I had also included the ship's control, so I was in fact a helmsman as well. I also went on regular tube space watch and ensured the weapons system was consistently maintained.

WHAT OPERATIONS WERE YOU INVOLVED IN?

Submarines in the Cold War era were constantly on the look out for Soviet submarines, and in fact any other submarines. If we came across them we would record their sound and follow them as far as the rules of engagement would allow. We'd also practice in case the Cold War went hot by surveying ships' movements and gathering intelligence.

TELL US ABOUT THE HMS ALLIANCE'S 1958 REFIT?

Alliance was built for Far East operations during World War Two. She missed the end of the war, so by the time she was operational, it was the Cold War where other submarines became the enemy. Therefore, the Royal Navy submarines were streamlined in order to become quieter and more difficult to detect.

HOW DID DIESEL-ELECTRIC SUBMARINES COPE IN THE NUCLEAR AGE?

They were for a different purpose. Diesel-electric submarines are much quieter when they've dived compared with nuclear subs and are harder to detect. Diesel-electric submarines made excellent listening platforms but they were much, much slower.

A submarine was away from land for so long that all metalwork had to be done at sea

The Duke of Cambridge came aboard on 12 May 2014 to observe the inner workings of Britain's last surviving Second World War submarine

ALLIANCE

Rex Features

WHERE DO ALL THE ROYAL NAVY SUBMARINES COME FROM?

INSIDE THE LARGEST INDOOR SHIPBUILDING COMPLEX IN EUROPE

HMS Alliance is one of many submarines to have been born in the dock of Barrow-in-Furness. A town and seaport in Cumbria, it has provided submarines to the Royal Navy for over a century. The port originally produced all types of naval ships but it has been solely submarines since the 1960s. Construction and investment had since declined but there has been a rebirth of sorts in recent years. Now owned by defence and security firm BAE Systems, the Devonshire Dock Hall complex is receiving a £300 million refurbishment in an eight-year cash injection. The current class of submarine is known as Vanguard but the upgrade, known simply as the 'Successor Program', will usher in a new wave of developments intended to replace the Trident System. The addition of these plans to the new Queen Elizabeth class of aircraft carriers demonstrates how far the Royal Navy has come since the days of HMS Alliance.

Above: *The shipyard at Barrow-in-Furness as it is currently (left) and how it could look after the investment (right)*

FROM AMPHION TO UPHOLDER

THE RISE AND DEMISE OF DIESEL-ELECTRIC SUBMARINES IN THE ROYAL NAVY

When Britain's first nuclear powered submarine HMS Dreadnought was completed on the 17 April 1963, many assumed that it would mark the end of diesel-electric submarines like HMS Alliance. This was not to be however, and the Porpoise, Oberon and Upholder classes all followed the Alliance and its Amphion class. The Upholders in particular were a vast improvement. First commissioned in 1990, they were intended to be a new generation of submarine in post-Falklands Britain. The new fleet utilized two 16-cyclinder engines that had an immensely high power-to-weight ratio. Its weapons also packed a punch with upgraded wire-guided heavyweight torpedoes, anti-ship missiles and submarine mines. However, despite the modern technology, a cut in Royal Navy finances meant the four vessels were put up for sale within two years of their completion. A buyer was eventually found in 1998 as the whole class was purchased by the Royal Canadian Navy. They are still in service in Canada to this day as the UK focuses its efforts fully on nuclear submarines.

HMCS Windsor, part of the Upholder class purchased by Canada in 1998

On many missions such as Operation Frankton in 1942, canoes were taken out of the boat through the hatch and used to engage the enemy while the sub retreated to a safe distance. They can be seen here stowed away beneath the torpedoes (bottom right)

The larder had to be stocked full for long journeys submerged under the waves

CL.476

"THE PORPOISE, OBERON AND UPHOLDER CLASSES ALL FOLLOWED THE ALLIANCE AND ITS AMPHION CLASS, BRINGING VAST IMPROVEMENTS"

HMS ALLIANCE TIMELINE: THE UNUSUAL LIFESPAN OF A UNIQUE VESSEL

1945
Built to serve in the Far East against Imperial Japan, HMS Alliance is laid down in March and launched in July.

1947
After test cruises the submarine is completed and commissioned in May. However, by the time it is ready to see action, the war has already ended.

1958
In order to bring her up to speed with contemporary standards, Alliance is given an extended refit and overhaul, streamlining and modernizing the entire vessel.

1968
Runs aground on the Bembridge Ridge on the Isle of Wight in January but is repaired in time to participate in the NATO Exercise in the Mediterranean on 5 November.

1971
On the 30 September there is a battery-related explosion on board the Alliance that kills one member of the crew and injures 14 others.

1973
Taken out of active service in March to become a static display ship at HMS Dolphin, Gosport. It is now solely used for harbor training duties.

1979
The decision is taken by the Royal Navy to prepare the Alliance for permanent display. Her keel is strengthened so she can be lifted on to land.

1981
Preserved as a submarine memorial and museum ship at the Royal Navy Submarine Museum, she is an enduring monument to the 4,334 submariners who lost their lives on active duty for Britain in both world wars.

AIR

MESSERSCHMITT BF109G

122 The WWII plane that changed warfare

WESTLAND WESSEX

142 This chopper brought gas turbines to the battlefield

C-130 HERCULES

148 Climb inside this mammoth transport vehicle

> ## "DESPITE HAVING A 172-FOOT WINGSPAN, THE B-2'S RADAR SIGNATURE IS AN ASTOUNDING 0.1M2"

A-10 THUNDERBOLT II

150 Step on board the fearsome Warthog

RECORD BREAKER

136 What made the F-4 Phantom II so revolutionary?

B-52 STRATOFORTRESS

130 This Boeing is a modern classic that still captivates hearts

© Alamy

FIGHTER PLANES

Over 100 years of aerial combat has produced some of the most impressive and effective military technology

F-22 RAPTOR *1996*

Country: USA

A SPEED FREAK WITH AN ARSENAL TO MATCH

This current generation of fighter aircraft is only operated by the United States Air Force – no other nation can purchase the plane, by Federal law. Designed to operate as a stealth attack aircraft, the F-22 has seen action in the Gulf and is capable of achieving incredible speeds of around 1,500mph.

VICKERS FB *1914*

Country: UK

THE UK'S FIRST FIGHTER PLANE

The Vickers was the first purpose-built fighter plane to be produced and was part of the world's first official fighter squadron. It came with two seats, a .303 Lewis gun and interestingly enough was only capable of speeds of around 70mph when at altitude.

POLIKARPOV I-15 *1934*

Country: Soviet Union

THE BACKBONE OF THE EARLY SOVIET AIR FORCE

The I-15 was used extensively from the 1930s to the mid-1940s by a selection of different nations. Flown by the Republicans during the Spanish Civil War, it remained in active service for many years, but was relegated to a ground-attack plane by 1941.

MESSERSCHMITT BF 109 *1935*

Country: Germany
NAZI GERMANY'S ALL-CONQUERING TECHNICAL MARVEL

Perhaps the most-feared aircraft of the Second World War, the Bf 109 was the scourge of the skies on the Western Front. Early versions actually saw action during the Spanish Civil War, and over 30,000 had been produced by the end of the European theater in 1945.

SOPWITH CAMEL *1916*

Country: UK
AN ICON OF THE SKIES OVER WWI EUROPE

A staple of the Royal Flying Corps during the First World War, the Sopwith Camel is perhaps the best-known aircraft of that era. Credited with a large number of confirmed kills, it became the most-prolific aircraft in Britain's arsenal, despite claims it was extremely difficult to fly.

F-16 FIGHTING FALCON *1975*

Country: USA
AMERICA'S MULTI-PURPOSE KILLER BIRD OF PREY

Used by a multitude of nations, the F-16 became one of the most widely deployed attack aircraft in the final decades of the 20th Century. The fighter has enjoyed varying military applications since its inception, and carries with it a fearsome arsenal for engaging targets at sea, on land or in dogfights.

TORNADO *1979*

Country: UK
STURDY BRITISH ENGINEERING AT ITS BEST

The Tornado was designed with both reconnaissance functionality and combat versatility in mind, with an array of features that enable it to perform effectively in all weather conditions, whether during the day or at night. It has seen action all over the world, notably during the First Gulf War.

5 Facts about FIGHTER PLANES

HESS TAKES FLIGHT

In 1941, deputy Führer Rudolph Hess hopped into a Bf 110 and flew to Scotland in an apparent attempt to open talks with Great Britain. The tail-end of his aircraft is on display at the Imperial War Museum.

DEATH FROM ABOVE

The monstrous GAU-8 cannon utilized by the A-10 Warthog generates so much recoil that if it weren't mounted off-center it would actually pull the plane off course while firing.

WINGING IT

In 1983 an Israeli pilot actually managed to land his F-15 despite it only having one wing. Apparently he was unaware of the extent of the damage that had been done to his plane.

OUTNUMBERED AND OUTGUNNED

During the Second World War, an American P-51 fighter managed to hold off around 30 German fighters that were attempting to down a flight of B-17s. This lasted for over half an hour.

THE PLANE OF THE FUTURE

The Eurofighter Typhoon attack aircraft is so advanced that it requires a series of computers to keep it airborne – a human being cannot pilot the Typhoon without their support.

The Eurofighter Typhoon can reach a maximum velocity of Mach 2.0

FIGHTER PLANES OF THE WORLD

We salute the most iconic fighters from around the globe

❶ LARGEST EVER DOGFIGHT

SYRIA 9 JUNE 1982

Nearly 200 fighter jets from Israel and Syria take to the skies and become embroiled in the largest air battle of all time. 80 Syrian planes are shot down.

Curtiss P-40
Produced: 1938
Speciality: Air superiority and ground attack
Location: USA

JAS 39 Gripen
Produced: 1988
Speciality: Strikes and recon
Location: Sweden

VL Myrsky
Produced: 1941
Speciality: Combat maneuvers
Location: Finland

P-51 Mustang
Produced: 1941
Speciality: High-speed attack fighter
Location: USA

AV-8B Harrier II
Produced: 1978
Speciality: V/STOL strike aircraft
Location: United Kingdom

❷

❽

❻

❶

Fiat CR.42
Produced: 1938
Speciality: Single-seat biplane
Location: Italy

IAR 80
Produced: 1941
Speciality: Ground attack aircraft
Location: Romania

❺

Dassault Mirage
Produced: 1967
Speciality: Ground attack fighter
Location: France

F2H Banshee
Produced: 1947
Speciality: Carrier-based jet fighter
Location: USA

F-14 Tomcat
Produced: 1969
Speciality: Long-range interceptor
Location: USA

343

❷ RAIDING OCCUPIED FRANCE

DIEPPE, FRANCE 19 AUGUST 1942

As part of a major Allied counter-offensive into occupied France, 74 aerial squadrons support ground troops during the Dieppe Raid. It's a failure, with scores of Spitfires and Hurricanes lost.

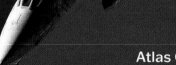

Atlas Cheetah
Produced: 1986
Speciality: All-round strike aircraft
Location: South Africa

❹

❸ SOVIET AIR SUPERIORITY
NORTH KOREA 12 APRIL 1951

Three squadrons of MiGs attack a flight of American B-29s in the midst of the Korean War without any Soviet losses. An embarrassed USAF christens the event Black Thursday.

MiG-29
Produced: 1977
Speciality: Short-range dogfighter
Location: Soviet Union

Ford Island was the epicenter of the Pearl Harbor attack

HESA Saeqeh
Produced: 2004
Speciality: Air battles and bombing runs
Location: Iran

❸

❼

Shenyang J-11
Produced: 1998
Speciality: Air superiority fighter
Location: China

❺ JAPAN STRIKES THE US
HAWAII 7 DECEMBER 1941

The Imperial Japanese Navy launches a surprise aerial attack on the US naval base at Pearl Harbor, sinking four Navy battleships and directly pressuring the US into intervening in the Second World War.

Mitsubishi A6M Zero
Produced: 1939
Speciality: Long-range dogfighter
Location: Japan

❻ WWI AIR BATTLE
ST. MIHIEL, EASTERN FRANCE
12 SEPTEMBER 1918

British and French planes take to the skies over France to engage Germany in one of the first major air-to-air battles of all time.

❼ CIVILIANS UNDER FIRE
ZHONGSHAN, CHINA
24 AUGUST 1938

A Douglas DC-2, the Kweilin, is shot down over China by Japanese aircraft. There are three survivors of what is considered the first instance of a civilian liner being downed by a fighter plane.

❽ DESERT STORM
IRAQ 17 JANUARY 1991

The first air-to-air victories of the First Gulf War are achieved. Two patrolling American F-15s shoot down and destroy two enemy Iraqi-operated MiG-29s. This is one of the first actions of Operation Desert Storm.

The Gulf War Allies sent hundreds of planes into Iraq

❹ BRITISH HARRIERS ATTACK
FALKLAND ISLANDS 5 MAY 1982

Three Sea Harriers from HMS Hermes launch a key attack on the Argentine airfield at Goose Green on the Falkland Islands with cluster bombs and 1,000lb bombs. One aircraft is lost to anti-aircraft fire.

ANATOMY OF A...
SPITFIRE

To this day the Spitfire is known across the globe as both a formidable weapon and a symbol of Britain's triumph in the skies

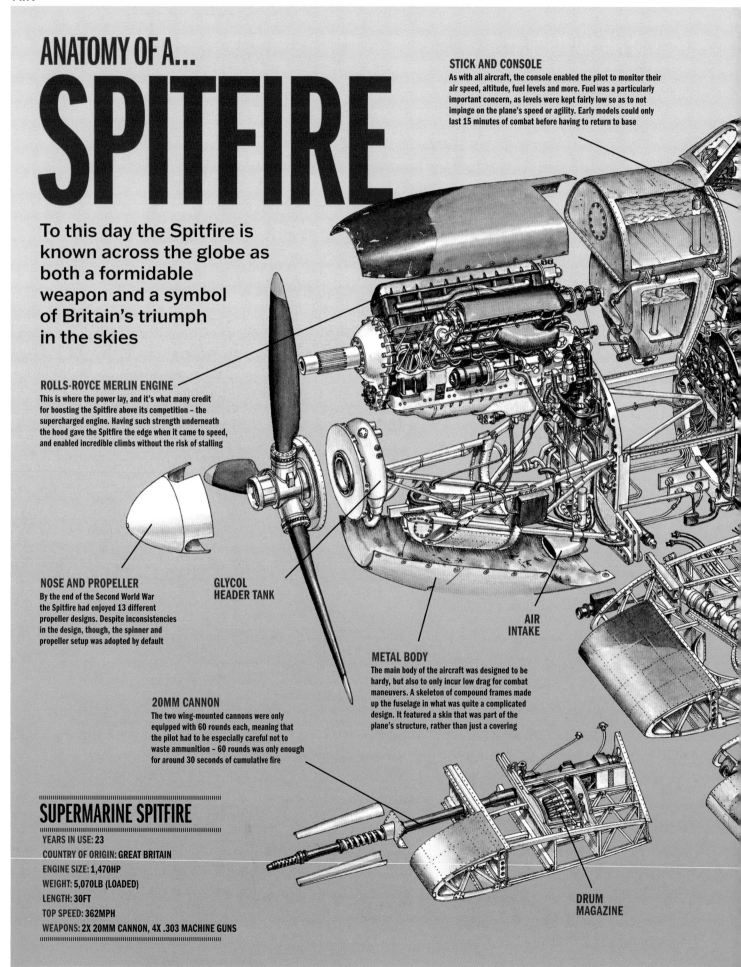

STICK AND CONSOLE

As with all aircraft, the console enabled the pilot to monitor their air speed, altitude, fuel levels and more. Fuel was a particularly important concern, as levels were kept fairly low so as to not impinge on the plane's speed or agility. Early models could only last 15 minutes of combat before having to return to base

ROLLS-ROYCE MERLIN ENGINE

This is where the power lay, and it's what many credit for boosting the Spitfire above its competition – the supercharged engine. Having such strength underneath the hood gave the Spitfire the edge when it came to speed, and enabled incredible climbs without the risk of stalling

NOSE AND PROPELLER

By the end of the Second World War the Spitfire had enjoyed 13 different propeller designs. Despite inconsistencies in the design, though, the spinner and propeller setup was adopted by default

GLYCOL HEADER TANK

AIR INTAKE

METAL BODY

The main body of the aircraft was designed to be hardy, but also to only incur low drag for combat maneuvers. A skeleton of compound frames made up the fuselage in what was quite a complicated design. It featured a skin that was part of the plane's structure, rather than just a covering

20MM CANNON

The two wing-mounted cannons were only equipped with 60 rounds each, meaning that the pilot had to be especially careful not to waste ammunition – 60 rounds was only enough for around 30 seconds of cumulative fire

DRUM MAGAZINE

SUPERMARINE SPITFIRE

YEARS IN USE: 23
COUNTRY OF ORIGIN: GREAT BRITAIN
ENGINE SIZE: 1,470HP
WEIGHT: 5,070LB (LOADED)
LENGTH: 30FT
TOP SPEED: 362MPH
WEAPONS: 2X 20MM CANNON, 4X .303 MACHINE GUNS

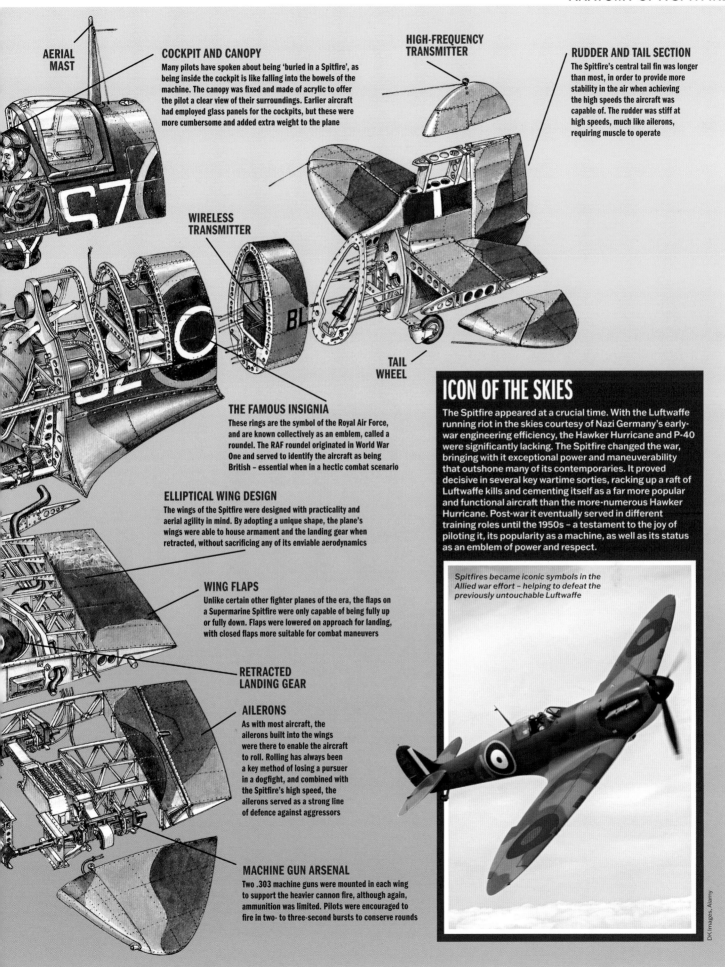

AERIAL MAST

COCKPIT AND CANOPY

Many pilots have spoken about being 'buried in a Spitfire', as being inside the cockpit is like falling into the bowels of the machine. The canopy was fixed and made of acrylic to offer the pilot a clear view of their surroundings. Earlier aircraft had employed glass panels for the cockpits, but these were more cumbersome and added extra weight to the plane

HIGH-FREQUENCY TRANSMITTER

RUDDER AND TAIL SECTION

The Spitfire's central tail fin was longer than most, in order to provide more stability in the air when achieving the high speeds the aircraft was capable of. The rudder was stiff at high speeds, much like ailerons, requiring muscle to operate

WIRELESS TRANSMITTER

TAIL WHEEL

THE FAMOUS INSIGNIA

These rings are the symbol of the Royal Air Force, and are known collectively as an emblem, called a roundel. The RAF roundel originated in World War One and served to identify the aircraft as being British – essential when in a hectic combat scenario

ELLIPTICAL WING DESIGN

The wings of the Spitfire were designed with practicality and aerial agility in mind. By adopting a unique shape, the plane's wings were able to house armament and the landing gear when retracted, without sacrificing any of its enviable aerodynamics

WING FLAPS

Unlike certain other fighter planes of the era, the flaps on a Supermarine Spitfire were only capable of being fully up or fully down. Flaps were lowered on approach for landing, with closed flaps more suitable for combat maneuvers

RETRACTED LANDING GEAR

AILERONS

As with most aircraft, the ailerons built into the wings were there to enable the aircraft to roll. Rolling has always been a key method of losing a pursuer in a dogfight, and combined with the Spitfire's high speed, the ailerons served as a strong line of defence against aggressors

MACHINE GUN ARSENAL

Two .303 machine guns were mounted in each wing to support the heavier cannon fire, although again, ammunition was limited. Pilots were encouraged to fire in two- to three-second bursts to conserve rounds

ICON OF THE SKIES

The Spitfire appeared at a crucial time. With the Luftwaffe running riot in the skies courtesy of Nazi Germany's early-war engineering efficiency, the Hawker Hurricane and P-40 were significantly lacking. The Spitfire changed the war, bringing with it exceptional power and maneuverability that outshone many of its contemporaries. It proved decisive in several key wartime sorties, racking up a raft of Luftwaffe kills and cementing itself as a far more popular and functional aircraft than the more-numerous Hawker Hurricane. Post-war it eventually served in different training roles until the 1950s – a testament to the joy of piloting it, its popularity as a machine, as well as its status as an emblem of power and respect.

Spitfires became iconic symbols in the Allied war effort – helping to defeat the previously untouchable Luftwaffe

DK Images, Alamy

BECOME A
TOP GUN

From cockpit layout to combat maneuvers, discover
what it takes to fly a fighter jet

The life of a fighter pilot requires courage, commitment and energy. While flying one of the most complex military machines in the world, monitoring and manipulating multiple systems, a pilot's training, intelligence and sharply honed skills work seamlessly. However, pilots never stop learning, growing and pushing themselves to the limit – both physically and mentally. "Complete dedication is required outside the cockpit too," says US Navy Lieutenant Joshua S Bettis. "The choice to fly jets for the Navy is life-consuming. The jets are expensive and dangerous. So, when a pilot isn't actually flying he is practising flying or studying. The current ratio of maintenance hours per flight hour also means that many sailors spend long days preparing jets to fly for short periods. In a training environment,

if a slip-up doesn't end in a mishap, it will affect a pilot's grades. There is seemingly an inexhaustible supply of young officers that would jump at the opportunity to take his spot."Fighter pilot training is intense and ongoing. Young jet pilot candidates complete initial flight screening in propeller-driven aircraft such as the Cessna 172. US Navy pilots progress through primary and advanced flight training, familiarizing themselves with additional aircraft such as the conventional Beechcraft T-34C Turbomentor and the McDonnell Douglas/ Boeing T-45C two-seat advanced jet trainer. Fighter pilots complete up to three years of training before earning their wings. During that time they spend countless hours in the classroom, respond to emergency situations in the simulator and endure the centrifuge, which spins the pilot vigorously

to replicate the intense G-forces they will encounter during the majority of in-flight maneuvers."The training we receive is everything from basic airmanship to air-to-ground munitions delivery and air-to-air combat," explains Lieutenant Commander Josh Denning. "We also train to land on aircraft carriers and refuel in flight. Flying is hard work. It requires hours of preparation for each flight. A typical 1.5-hour flight would consist of approximately two hours of briefing before the flight, the flight itself, and then anywhere from one hour to many hours for a debrief of the event." Navy fighter pilots are constantly reminded that the success of a mission depends on them. Once they've mastered a fighter capable of flashing into combat at more than 994 mi per hour, a pilot must be ready to spring into action at a moment's notice.

FLIGHT GEAR

FIGHTER PILOTS REQUIRE SPECIALIST EQUIPMENT TO TACKLE DEATH-DEFYING MANEUVERS

Suiting up is a critical aspect of the job. Fighter pilots' equipment is often tailored to their mission, whether the jet aircraft is flying faster than the speed of sound, engaging hostile targets or even if the pilot is on the ground, evading capture or fighting for survival.

"A pilot wears a helmet and visor, a mask which is worn at all times with a radio incorporated, a flight suit made from aramid (Nomex) – a material that is not fireproof but will char instead of melt – gloves, steel-toed boots, a G-suit, harness and survival vest," explains Lieutenant Bettis. "Other types of equipment vary depending on your mission, whether it is peacetime training or combat."

The flight suit is ideal for protecting the fighter pilot in case of an onboard fire. "It's like zip-up pajamas with a few pockets. It's pretty simple," Bettis describes. "The G-suit, on the other hand, is an expensive piece of gear that plugs into a receptacle in the cockpit." Heavy acceleration can generate high G-forces on the pilot, sending blood rushing towards their head or their feet. Either scenario can cause a pilot to pass out, so pressurized G-suits are worn to combat this.

In cold weather, pilots don a rubber-lined exposure suit that functions much like a diver's wetsuit, providing insulation and retaining body warmth if they land in water after a forced ejection. Gloves are made of Nomex material similar to the flight suit,

and are both fire-resistant and warm in cold weather.

"We carry a large assortment of mostly survival gear on our vest," explains Lieutenant Commander Denning, "in case we ever have to eject." The survival vest contains a hand-held GPS for orientation, waterproof matches, thimble-like lights that turn fingertips into miniature flashlights, camouflage paint, a tourniquet for wound treatment, and more.

Every pilot's outfit is meticulously thought out for their safety

NEXT-GEN HELMETS

WHAT TECH MAKES THE F-35 GEN III INTO A PILOT'S ULTIMATE WINGMAN?

QUIET FLIGHT
Active noise reduction allows the pilot to focus and operate the F-35 in flight with minimal distractions

NIGHT VISION
Integrated digital night vision technology provides superior awareness while flying in heavy darkness

CAMERA
Video recording helps to monitor the pilots' performance on missions and even identifies training opportunities

BLIND SPOTS
The headset provides a wide, unrestricted field of view, giving the pilot a clear view of their setting

VISOR
The F-35 pilot's $400,000 visor functions as a head-up display with six high-res cameras embedded on the outside of the plane

LIGHTWEIGHT
The F-35 helmet shell is constructed of carbon graphite, reducing weight to 5 pounds

PRECISE FIT
A pupilometer calculates the distance between the pilot's eyes, and a dozen other measurements help provide an exact fit. This avoids the helmet causing motion sickness in flight

G-SUIT INTEGRATION
Custom fitted hoses and cables, integrated with the pilot's G-suit, allow freedom of movement

The flight suit's transparent thigh pockets usually hold the flight plan and a map

MEET THE PILOTS

LIEUTENANT JOSHUA S BETTIS, US NAVY

Lieutenant Bettis graduated from the US Naval Academy in 2006 and was designated a student naval aviator. He earned his wings in 2009, subsequently serving with Squadron VFA-125 in Lemoore, California, flying the F/A-18C Hornet fighter. In 2011, he transitioned to the Civil Engineer Corps and currently serves with Naval Facilities Engineering Command in Washington, DC.

LIEUTENANT COMMANDER JOSH DENNING, US NAVAL RESERVE

Lieutenant Commander Josh Denning was commissioned in the US Navy through Officer Candidate School in 2007. He earned his wings in 2009, serving at naval air stations in Florida, Texas, and California. He flew the F/A-18E and F/A-18F Hornet fighters. He works as a police officer and as a reserve staff supply officer for the Seventh Fleet.

IN THE COCKPIT

THE FIGHTER PILOT MONITORS AND OPERATES SCORES OF SWITCHES, CONTROLS AND BUTTONS

"A SPLIT SECOND COULD BE THE DIFFERENCE BETWEEN BEING THE HUNTER OR THE HUNTED"

During all phases of operation, pre-flight, in-flight, and post-flight, the fighter pilot is constantly aware of their surroundings, and the command center of the jet aircraft is the cockpit. To those who have not trained as pilots, the confusing mass of control panels is overwhelming, but to seasoned professionals the operation of these instruments is second nature, thanks to years of training.

"Pilots develop a cockpit scan over time, where each instrument is monitored at an appropriate interval," relates Lieutenant Joshua Bettis. "The scan varies depending on the pilot's mission. Pilots also spend a

significant amount of time in the books. They must know the proper use and limitations of every piece of gear on the jet."

Today's fighter jets are configured for a variety of missions, engaging in air superiority operations and ground targeting. "Everything in the cockpit is as streamlined as possible for the pilot to operate the systems, their hands never leaving the controls," says Lieutenant Commander Josh Denning. "Before we even learn to fly airplanes we go through many hours of cockpit familiarization, learning the systems and their respective

controls in the cockpit."

The pilot has to know their stuff when a split second could be the difference between being the hunter or the hunted. "Training depends on the complexity of the gear the pilot is learning," Bettis continues. "Ground school covers complex instrument function and theory, followed by simulators with seasoned instructor pilots. Next, the instruments are utilized in maneuvers and tactics in the aircraft – normally in a 'demo-do' format, where the instructor demonstrates proper usage before the student makes an attempt."

STAYING IN CONTROL
FIGHTER PILOTS MUST KNOW THEIR COCKPIT LAYOUT AND THE FUNCTION OF EVERY CONSOLE IN IT

CANOPY VIEW
The HUD combiner glass provides the pilot with the head-up display that shows critical data

TELEVISION
The television sensor supplies real-time images for the pilot to monitor and react to

AIRSPEED INDICATOR
The airspeed indicator tells the pilot how fast they are flying at all times

FUEL INDICATOR
The fuel quantity indicator allows the pilot to assess flight time and distance

CHAFF/FLARE CONTROL PANEL
Electronic countermeasures allow the jet fighter to jam enemy radar signals and prevent hostile missiles

THROTTLE
The throttle controls the starting and stopping of the engine, along with manual controls for communications and other systems

ELECTRICAL PANEL
The pilot can control whether the fighter jet is powered by its generator or battery. The Emergency Power Unit can provide power for an hour in the event of an engine failure

TEST PANEL
On the test panel, switches and buttons can be used to test circuits, lights, onboard computers, warning systems and numerous other measurements too

ENGINE CONTROLS
Engine controls are used to manipulate the jet fuel starter system and computerized engine functions

Scores of knobs, buttons and switches govern the function of at least 20 systems, each of them critical to the fighter's performance and the survival of the pilot. These include the engine, along with other systems related to fuel, environment and temperature, electrical systems, flight control, hydraulics, landing gear, autopilot, lighting, communications, navigation, IFF (Identification, Friend or Foe), weapons, radar and more. "As pilots progress in their careers and aircraft get more expensive to fly, the learning curve gets steeper,"

explains Lieutenant Bettis. "Students work through 20 or more flights in primary flight training just to be able to solo a T-34C. Conversely, a newly winged aviator that is transitioning into the Hornet is expected to solo on his third or fourth flight. Simulators are an excellent tool used to teach pilots and evaluate their performance in a low risk setting. They allow instructors to create emergency situations that otherwise wouldn't be feasible, and adjust conditions such as weather to challenge a pilot that is working on instrument flight."

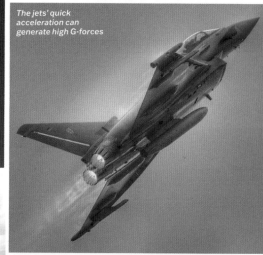

The jets' quick acceleration can generate high G-forces

ALL GOOD IN THE HUD

THE HEAD-UP DISPLAY SHOWS PILOTS THEIR ESSENTIAL REAL-TIME DATA

The fighter jet head-up display (HUD) presents data to the pilot in their forward field of view through the integration of three basic components: the projector unit, combiner and video generation computer. This setup means they don't have to divert their eyes while in flight, which minimizes the distractions of looking down or away from the front of the aircraft, and avoids the pilot having to refocus their eyesight when assessing data. A typical HUD provides the airspeed, altitude, horizon line and global positioning, as well as navigational and aerial combat information. This includes data such as angle of attack, number of available weapons, range to target and whether or not they are locked onto an enemy aircraft.

Mastering the cockpit controls of a fighter jet takes years of training

The F-35B is specially designed to take off over short distances

AIRSPEED SCALE
The airspeed scale indicates the current speed of the fighter plane in knots

HORIZON LINE
The horizon line indicates the orientation of the plane with respect to the horizon in the pilot's line of sight

FLIGHT PATH MARKER
This corresponds to the flight path or vector that the pilot has set

GUN CROSS
The gun cross shows where the nose of the aircraft is currently pointing

NUCLEAR CONSENT SWITCH
If nuclear weapons are carried, manipulating this switch gives the jet consent to arm and release them

PITCH ATTITUDE BARS
Pitch attitude bars show whether the jet's nose is tilted up or down

IN FLIGHT

WITH GREAT POWER COMES GREAT RESPONSIBILITY: HOW TO HANDLE A FIGHTER JET LIKE A PRO

Few fighter pilots would deny that the adrenaline rush of take-off, flight and landing is exhilarating, but they are also clear that the experience comes with significant responsibility. "Inside the cockpit there can be no complacency," warns Lieutenant Bettis. "Even the greatest pilots are one mistake away from demonstrating their mortality."

The fighter jet is designed for speed and maneuverability, and pilots feel they are on the aircraft rather than inside it, surrounded by the cockpit. "You literally strap the plane on to you," says David Collette, a former F-16 pilot in the US Air Force. "The plane is your life, but you are the brain." In contrast to the wrangling of a fighter jet, commercial aircraft are designed for stability, a smooth ride and passenger comfort. In a fighter jet there are no passengers, just highly skilled professionals who are trained to complete dangerous missions. The fighter jet accelerates like a race car, and the characteristics of the aircraft shape and mould the flight experience. The shake of turbulence is never cushioned. "Flying a fighter is the most exhilarating feeling I have ever had," explains Lieutenant Commander Denning. "There is an absolute sense of freedom while flying, especially in a high performance airplane such as the Hornet. G-forces feel as if you have weight pressing down on every part of your body. It takes a lot of practice to master the physiology of fighting the forces you experience in the cockpit to maintain consciousness and continue your mission. It is a very intense workout, and sweating out as much as five pounds of body weight is not uncommon under our most physically stressful missions."

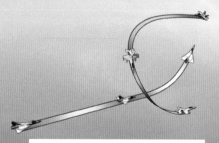

The F-22 Raptor can cruise at supersonic speeds

THE FORCE IS STRONG

THE HEAD-UP DISPLAY SHOWS PILOTS THEIR ESSENTIAL REAL-TIME DATA

Tight turns, steep dives and swift climbs are all in a day's work for the fighter pilot, and the laws of physics take their toll. The power of gravity exerted on the human body during acceleration, deceleration and turning is known as G-force (G). Standing still you experience 1G under gravitational pressure, but when flying, the Gs that pilots feel are directly proportional to the jet's changing velocity. Ordinary activities like riding a roller coaster, or heavily accelerating or braking in a car, could generate up to 3Gs. Fighter pilots, flying at tremendous speeds may 'pull' up to 9Gs, restricting the normal flow of blood and potentially causing a blackout. During maneuvers the pilot is at great risk when blood pools in the lower extremities and the brain is starved of oxygen. To ward off the effects of G-forces, pilots wear a G-suit that provides a continuous flow of air, operating like a large blood pressure cuff.

A US Marine Corps fighter pilot dons gear, including the G-suit, prior to a mission

AERIAL COMBAT MANEUVERS

FIGHTER PILOTS EXECUTE PRECISE MOVES TO GAIN THE DECISIVE EDGE ON AN ADVERSARY

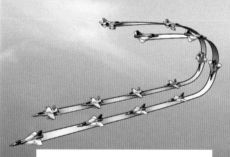

TURNING IN
A pilot seeking the most advantageous firing position on the tail of their adversary may execute this turn to close in

LEAD TURN
This move enables a pursuing fighter pilot to close in on their opponent by starting to turn before the planes pass each other

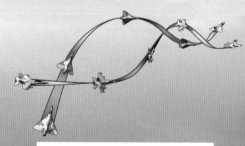

ROLLING SCISSORS
Often following a high-speed overshoot, an evader reverses into a vertical climb and barrel roll, compelling the pursuer to follow

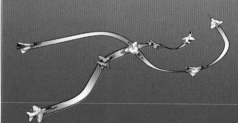

FLAT SCISSORS
This maneuver involves two planes weaving from side to side as they each try to get behind the other

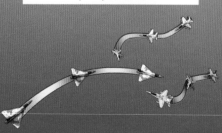

BRACKET
Two pursuers launching a pincer attack force the evader to choose which opponent they will engage in combat

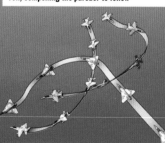

HOOK-AND-DRAG
Two pursuers launching a pincer attack can take advantage of an evader's turn towards either of them to follow up with an attack

SAFETY FIRST

FIGHTER PILOTS MUST BE VIGILANT AT ALL TIMES

The warning light flashes. Sights, sounds and sensors alert of potential disaster. Instinctively, the pilot takes action, as safety is second nature. Then, the exercise is over. The flight simulator has done its job so the pilot will know how to do theirs. "The simulators are run by former pilots with a breadth and depth of experience," remarks Lieutenant Bettis. "However, nothing replaces seat time in the jet," he adds.

During that "seat time" the pilot is constantly alert, blending their knowledge with onboard systems that keep both pilot and plane safe. Flying is a risky business. Not only does the pilot's life depend on it, the fate of a jet aircraft worth millions is also in their hands.

"Flying an airplane like the Hornet demands 100 percent of your focus and situational awareness for 100 percent of the time," relates Lieutenant Commander Denning. "Flying is terribly unforgiving for any carelessness, incapacity or neglect. There are systems in the airplane that alert us to several different types of emergencies, but most importantly it's the focus you must maintain that keeps a pilot safe."

Safety begins with pilot awareness and follows established procedures. From suiting up with indispensable gear to a huge range of pre-flight checks, the pilot works to minimize risk, through take-off, mission fulfilment and landing.

Ejecting is always a last resort for fighter pilots

"FLYING A FIGHTER IS THE MOST EXHILARATING FEELING I HAVE EVER HAD" – LIEUTENANT COMMANDER DENNING

THE LAST RESORT

PILOTS ONLY EJECT FROM THEIR JETS WHEN ALL OTHER OPTIONS ARE EXHAUSTED

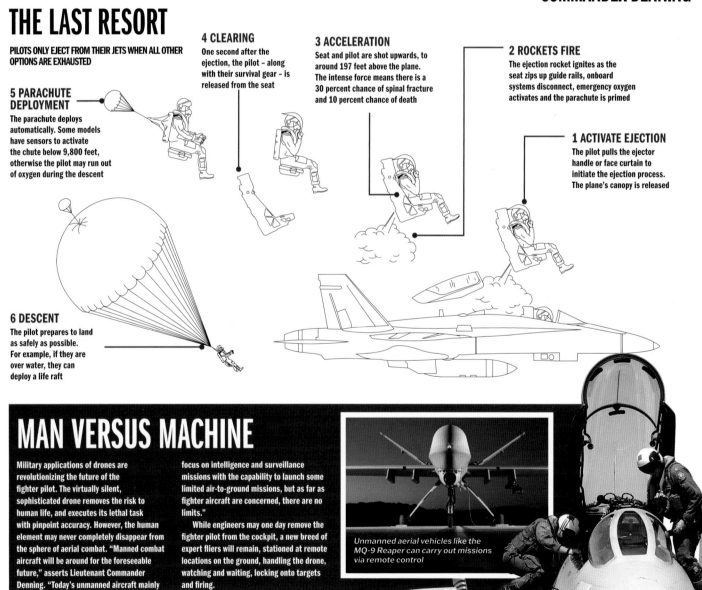

4 CLEARING
One second after the ejection, the pilot – along with their survival gear – is released from the seat

3 ACCELERATION
Seat and pilot are shot upwards, to around 197 feet above the plane. The intense force means there is a 30 percent chance of spinal fracture and 10 percent chance of death

2 ROCKETS FIRE
The ejection rocket ignites as the seat zips up guide rails, onboard systems disconnect, emergency oxygen activates and the parachute is primed

5 PARACHUTE DEPLOYMENT
The parachute deploys automatically. Some models have sensors to activate the chute below 9,800 feet, otherwise the pilot may run out of oxygen during the descent

1 ACTIVATE EJECTION
The pilot pulls the ejector handle or face curtain to initiate the ejection process. The plane's canopy is released

6 DESCENT
The pilot prepares to land as safely as possible. For example, if they are over water, they can deploy a life raft

MAN VERSUS MACHINE

Military applications of drones are revolutionizing the future of the fighter pilot. The virtually silent, sophisticated drone removes the risk to human life, and executes its lethal task with pinpoint accuracy. However, the human element may never completely disappear from the sphere of aerial combat. "Manned combat aircraft will be around for the foreseeable future," asserts Lieutenant Commander Denning. "Today's unmanned aircraft mainly focus on intelligence and surveillance missions with the capability to launch some limited air-to-ground missions, but as far as fighter aircraft are concerned, there are no limits."

While engineers may one day remove the fighter pilot from the cockpit, a new breed of expert fliers will remain, stationed at remote locations on the ground, handling the drone, watching and waiting, locking onto targets and firing.

Unmanned aerial vehicles like the MQ-9 Reaper can carry out missions via remote control

MESSERSCHMITT

Take a tour around one of World War II's most iconic aircraft and the backbone of the Third Reich's Luftwaffe

The aircraft seen here is an accurate replica of a 1943 Bf 109G-6, with the unique pattern used by Hermann Graf of JG.50 – he ended the war with 212 confirmed victories in the air

MESSERSCHMITT BF 109G

CREW: **1**		MAX TAKEOFF WEIGHT: **7,495LB**	
LENGTH: **29FT 7IN**		POWERPLANT: **1 x DAIMLER-BENZ DB 605A-1 LIQUID-COOLED INVERTED V12, 1,455HP**	
WINGSPAN: **32FT 6IN**			
HEIGHT: **8FT 2IN**			
WING AREA: **173.3FT²**		PROPELLERS: **VDM 9-12087 THREE-BLADED LIGHT-ALLOY PROPELLER**	
EMPTY WEIGHT: **5,893LB**			
LOADED WEIGHT: **6,940LB**		PROPELLER DIAMETER: **9FT 10IN**	

BF 109G

Right: Though designed as a short range interceptor, Bf 109 variants served in many roles across all fronts

"WHILE ULTIMATELY NOT THE VERY BEST FIGHTING PLATFORM BY 1945, IT WAS BUILT IN HUGE NUMBERS, WITH MORE THAN 33,000 CONSTRUCTED BETWEEN 1937 AND 1945"

Fighting against its arch rival the Supermarine Spitfire, the Messerschmitt Bf 109 is probably the most famous Axis fighter of World War II. In the early years of the war, it was the main single-engine fighter interceptor of the Luftwaffe. While the E variant began to be outclassed by the Spitfire Mk IX after the Battle of Britain and was eventually replaced by the Focke Wulf 190, the Bf 109 in fact continued to serve across all fronts of German combat right until the war's end. While ultimately not the very

best fighting platform by 1945, it was built in huge numbers, with more than 33,000 constructed between 1937 and 1945. The most numerous variant was the Bf 109G, with more than a third of all aircraft being this specification.

Originally designed as a short-range, high-speed, extremely agile interceptor, the Bf 109 was built in response to a tender by the German Reich Aviation Ministry in 1933. It was one of several specifications laid out by the Reich at the time that formed the future of the Luftwaffe as Germany prepared for war. Heinkel, Arado,

BFW and Focke Wulf all competed for the contract. The specification was for a fighter with a top speed of more than 248.5 miles per hour at 20,000 feet but with a flight endurance of only 90 minutes. The German Blitzkrieg warfare tactics at the time anticipated that close air support behind the main advancing front would be the main area of operations.

The Bf 109 made its debut in 1935 and played an active part in the Spanish Civil War, something that gave Luftwaffe pilots a crucial initial edge of combat experience at the outset of World War II.

AIR

DESIGN

The Bf 109 initially had a 700-horsepower Jumo V12, but when the prototypes were ready, the engines were behind schedule. The Bf 109 at first flew with a Rolls-Royce Kestrel engine, acquired by trading a Heinkel aircraft with Rolls-Royce, who needed an engine test bed.

Other advanced technologies included leading edge slats that deployed automatically to enhance combat manoeuvering. Early test pilots were wary of the design, with on-the-limit handling in steep combat turns becoming tricky. However, once mastered, the agility gave it an edge in air-to-air combat. Other elements that pilots disliked were the undercarriage arrangement and the fact that the canopy was designed to open sideways rather then slide back, meaning that it could not be opened in flight.

However, there is little doubt that the Messerschmitt was designed to survive combat. The engine was inverted, making it more difficult to damage by ground fire, while also giving the aircraft the ability to undertake negative-G maneuvers in ways that Merlin-engined aircraft could not follow. The radiators had two separate systems that could be shut off independently in the event of damage, which allowed the pilot to continue flying. The aircraft would even continue to fly for five minutes with no radiators, giving the pilot a chance to escape from a dogfight if damaged.

Additionally, the fuselage fuel tank was behind the pilot and also behind the armor plating, reducing the possibility of penetration by gunfire and also burns to the pilot.

The initial Jumo engines were underpowered, with the Daimler-Benz engine eventually replacing it in a major redesign of the E series. The Bf 109E 'Emil' had major structural changes to accommodate the 1,100-horsepower Daimler-Benz engine. This model formed the basis for the G 'Gustav' series from 1942 onwards.

The design by Willy Messerschmitt used cutting-edge technologies at the time to create an extremely light monoplane design. Wherever possible, the number of components was minimized, with load-bearing structures such as engine and wing mounts being combined into one assembly. The unusual aircraft landing gear was also mounted on the same structure, which gave rise to the rather odd looking stance when on the ground. While it made the aircraft difficult to handle in landing and takeoff, it did allow the wings to be quickly removed with the gear in place, making for rapid battle damage repairs. The engine was a liquid-cooled V12, running inverted with the exhaust stacks at the bottom of the cowlings.

The unusual undercarriage layout made the Messerschmitt tricky to handle on the ground

"THE DESIGN BY WILLY MESSERSCHMITT USED CUTTING-EDGE TECHNOLOGIES AT THE TIME TO CREATE AN EXTREMELY LIGHT MONOPLANE DESIGN"

This 100 percent accurate replica of the Bf 109G can be seen on display at the Yorkshire Air Museum

Additional cannon were added as a field modification to improve armament

PERFORMANCE

MAXIMUM SPEED: **398MPH AT 20,669FT**
CRUISE SPEED: **365MPH AT 19,680FT**
RANGE: **28MI, 621MI WITH DROP TANK**
SERVICE CEILING: **39,370FT**
RATE OF CLIMB: **56FT/S**
WING LOADING: **40LB/FT²**
POWER/MASS: **0.21HP/LB**

POWERPLANT

The Bf 109G was powered by the Daimler-Benz DB605 liquid-cooled V12 engine. This developed 1,475 brake horsepower and was the engine that would power the Messerschmitt variants for the rest of the war. The engine was a V12, inverted, liquid-cooled engine developed as a high-performance version of the earlier DB601. To keep pace with Rolls-Royce Merlin advances, this engine was designed to rev higher and run with greater supercharger boost

than previously, while still remaining reliable in combat and not overheating. The supercharger clutch was automatic, as was the electric pitch control for the propeller, giving the pilot less to worry about in the stress of combat situations.

Aviation fuel is typically 100 octane, but Daimler-Benz designed the engines to run at reduced power on lower octane fuels, even as low as 87 octane. This meant that in frontline combat where aviation fuel may be scarce, the aircraft could continue fighting using whatever fuel could be found.

Vorsicht beim Öffnen
Kühler ist im Haubentiel eingebaut

The Daimler Benz liquid cooled inverted V12 was particularly robust and able to continue operating when damaged

ROLES AND DIVERSITY

Though originally designed solely as a short-range high-performance interceptor, the Bf 109G was pressed into service in other areas. In Africa and on the Soviet front, the aircraft was frequently used for ground attack, able to carry a single bomb centrally in addition to the cannon and machine guns carried onboard. As with the Allied Supermarine Spitfire, the Bf 109 was adapted for different roles and environments.

After the early A, B, C and D models, the Bf 109E was the first major overhaul, leading to the Gustav model here. A marine variant known as the T was produced in limited numbers, with additional small-scale productions of high-altitude photo-reconnaissance and even a two-seat trainer at various times.

"IN AFRICA AND ON THE RUSSIAN FRONT, THE AIRCRAFT WAS FREQUENTLY USED FOR GROUND ATTACK"

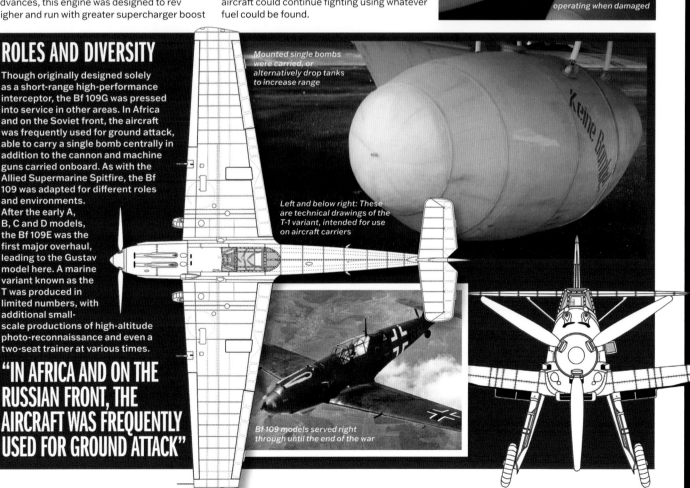

Mounted single bombs were carried, or alternatively drop tanks to increase range

Left and below right: These are technical drawings of the T-1 variant, intended for use on aircraft carriers

Bf 109 models served right through until the end of the war

The Bf109G had a central cannon firing through the propellor spinner

ACHTUNG

REVI

COCKPIT

The pilot sat in a seat designed to be used with a parachute. Armor plating behind him also covered the rear fuel tank for additional protection. Ahead was a bulletproof windscreen. The central-mounted cannon was also visible in the cockpit, which must have been deafening when in use. Pilots often criticized the cockpit canopy, both for the shallow frame that obscured vision and the fact that it hinged open sideways, meaning that it could not be opened in flight. In keeping with the compact design philosophy of Willy Messerschmitt, the cockpit was a tight fit.

Left: With a side-opening canopy, the cockpit was far harder to bail out of while in flight – an understandably unpopular feature with pilots

ARMAMENT

The thin, high-performance wing of the Messerschmitt Bf 109G meant that most of the armament was positioned centrally. Twin machine guns in the fuselage were supplemented by a 20mm cannon mounted in the center of the V12 engine. This fired through the center of the propeller spinner.

As the war progressed, this firepower was becoming ineffective, so the Luftwaffe introduced field modifications known as Rüstsätze. This was typically a kit capable of being retrofitted in the field by ground crew. Such kits were generally mounted under the wing and included payloads such as extra cannon for ground attack, machine-gun pods or drop tanks to increase the limited range. This gave the aircraft additional diversity to enable the fight to continue, in particular on the Russian Front and in Africa.

WEAPONS

GUNS: 2 x 0.51IN SYNCHRONISED MG 131 MACHINE GUNS WITH 300 ROUNDS PER GUN
1 x 0.78IN MG 151/20 CANNON WITH 200 ROUNDS PER GUN, OR
1 x 1.18IN MK 108 CANNON WITH 65 ROUNDS PER GUN (G-6/U4 VARIANT),
2 x 20MM MG 151/20 UNDER-WING CANNON PODS WITH 135 ROUNDS PER GUN (OPTIONAL KIT: RÜSTSÄTZE VI)
ROCKETS: 2 x 8IN WFR GR 21 ROCKETS (G-6 WITH BR21)
BOMBS: 1 x 551LB BOMB OR 4 x 110LB BOMBS OR 1 x 300-LITER DROP TANK

Top German fighter aces amassed hundreds of kills and sometimes had aircraft painted with their own colors

POST-WAR

A British soldier poses on top of a downed Bf 109 E, during the Battle of Britain

Almost 34,000 Messerschmitt Bf 109s were built from 1935 until 1945, yet only about 100 survive today. Many are static, though some are still in flying condition. Most of those that survive were either captured by the Allies at the end of the war or recovered from combat areas of Russia and Eastern Europe, where they were abandoned and lost in large numbers at the end of the war.

LANCASTER BOMBER

Famed for its prowess and entrenched in popular culture by *The Dam Busters* film of 1955, the Lancaster bomber played a vital role in securing an Allied victory in World War II

Arguably the most famous heavy bomber of World War II, the Avro-built Lancaster bomber undertook some of the most dangerous and complex missions yet encountered by the RAF. Primarily a night bomber but frequently used during the daytime too, the Lancasters under Bomber Command flew some 156,000 sorties during the war, dropping 609,000 tons of bombs. Among these bombs was the famous 'bouncing bomb' designed by British inventor Barnes Wallis, a payload that would lead the Lancaster to remain famed long after 1945. Take a look inside the famed Avro Lancaster to see what made it so successful.

Lancaster bombers dropped 609,000 tons of bombs

INSIDE A LANCASTER BOMBER

LANCASTER BOMBER

CREW 7
LENGTH 69FT
WINGSPAN 102FT
HEIGHT 24FT
WEIGHT 63,934LBS
POWERPLANT 4 X ROLLS-ROYCE MERLIN XX V12 ENGINES
MAX SPEED 280MPH
MAX RANGE 3,000 MILES
MAX ALTITUDE 26,771FT
ARMAMENT 8 X .7.7MM BROWNING MACHINE GUNS; BOMB LOAD OF 13,889LBS

CREW
Due to its large size, hefty armament and technical complexity, the Lancaster bomber had a crew of seven. This included: a pilot, flight engineer, navigator, bomb aimer, wireless operator, mid-upper and rear gunners. Many crew members from Lancasters were awarded the Victoria Cross for their heroic actions in battle, a notable example being the two awarded after a daring daytime raid on Augsburg, Germany

BOMB BAY
The bomb bay could carry a great payload. Indeed, the bay was so spacious that with a little modification it could house the massive Grand Slam "earthquake" bomb, a 22,046lb giant that when released would reach near sonic speeds before penetrating deep into the Earth and exploding

TURRETS
As standard the Lancaster bomber was fitted with three twin 7.7mm turrets in the nose, rear and upper-middle fuselage. In some later variants of the Lancaster the twin 7.7mm machine guns were replaced with 12.7mm models, which delivered more power. The rear and upper-middle turrets were staffed permanently by dedicated gunners, while the nose turret was staffed periodically by the bomb aimer when caught up in a dogfight

FUSELAGE
The Lancaster was designed out of the earlier Avro Type 683 Manchester III bomber, which sported a three-finned tail layout and was similar in construction. While the overall build remained similar the tri-fin was removed in favor of a twin-finned set up instead. This is famously one of only a small number of design alterations made to the bomber, which was deemed to be just right after its test flights

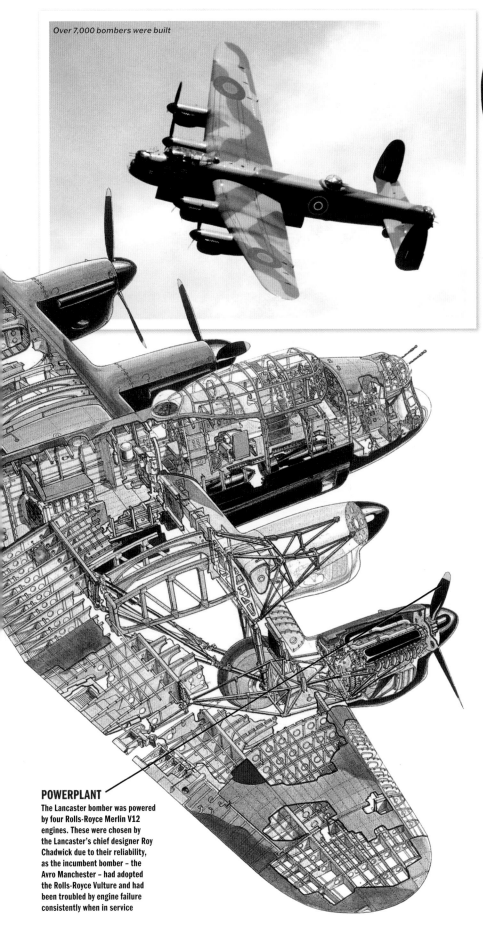

Over 7,000 bombers were built

POWERPLANT
The Lancaster bomber was powered by four Rolls-Royce Merlin V12 engines. These were chosen by the Lancaster's chief designer Roy Chadwick due to their reliability, as the incumbent bomber – the Avro Manchester – had adopted the Rolls-Royce Vulture and had been troubled by engine failure consistently when in service

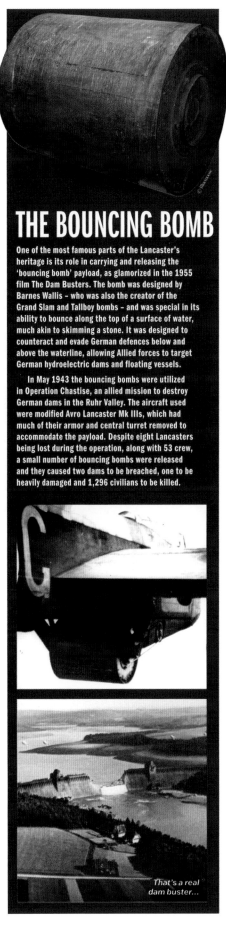

THE BOUNCING BOMB

One of the most famous parts of the Lancaster's heritage is its role in carrying and releasing the 'bouncing bomb' payload, as glamorized in the 1955 film The Dam Busters. The bomb was designed by Barnes Wallis – who was also the creator of the Grand Slam and Tallboy bombs – and was special in its ability to bounce along the top of a surface of water, much akin to skimming a stone. It was designed to counteract and evade German defences below and above the waterline, allowing Allied forces to target German hydroelectric dams and floating vessels.

In May 1943 the bouncing bombs were utilized in Operation Chastise, an allied mission to destroy German dams in the Ruhr Valley. The aircraft used were modified Avro Lancaster Mk IIIs, which had much of their armor and central turret removed to accommodate the payload. Despite eight Lancasters being lost during the operation, along with 53 crew, a small number of bouncing bombs were released and they caused two dams to be breached, one to be heavily damaged and 1,296 civilians to be killed.

That's a real dam buster...

BOEING B-52 STRATOFORTRESS

This iconic symbol of American air power is one of the oldest military aircraft in service today, and still a potent force to be reckoned with

The B-52 Stratofortress defines the era for which it was created: the Cold War. At a time when nuclear war threatened to destroy humanity, this aircraft acted as both the enabler of apocalyptic destruction and its deterrent. It is the ultimate heavy bomber, designed for sorties from a maximum height of 50,000 feet, primarily with nuclear weapons.

The craft has a total global reach, as it can be refuelled in midair, but what is most surprising is its age and flexibility. Although it is still one of the most feared weapons in the USA's arsenal, the first prototypes were ordered as far back as 1948, in the wake of WWII, with the first plane taking to the skies in April 1952.

The key to the B-52's success is its relative simplicity. Despite a huge airframe, it is not made from complex materials like carbon fiber, and as such it can adapt to many different modifications and parts can be easily repaired or replaced. The specific aircraft featured here was ordered in 1956 and first flew in 1957, becoming the 689th B-52 to enter service. It now resides in the American Air Museum as part of the Imperial War Museum Duxford.

Over 700 of the planes have been built and any B-52s that are in service today were built in the early 1960s. Engineering analyzes have shown that the B-52's operational lifespan could extend beyond 2040, an extraordinary achievement for an aircraft design that predates the Korean War.

"ALTHOUGH IT IS STILL ONE OF THE MOST FEARED WEAPONS IN THE USA'S ARSENAL, THE FIRST PROTOTYPES WERE ORDERED AS FAR BACK AS 1948, IN THE WAKE OF WWII, WITH THE FIRST PLANE TAKING TO THE SKIES IN APRIL 1952"

BOEING B-52 STRATOFORTRESS

POWER PLANT: 8 PRATT & WITNEY ENGINES TF33-P-3/103 TURBOFAN
THRUST: EACH ENGINE UP TO 17,000 LBS
WINGSPAN: 185 FT
WEIGHT: APPROX 185,000 LBS
FUEL CAPACITY: 312,197 LBS
SPEED: 650 MPH (MACH 0.86)
RANGE: 8,800 MI (7,652 NAUTICAL MILES)
CEILING: 50,000 FT
CREW: 5 (COMMANDER, PILOT, RADAR NAVIGATOR, NAVIGATOR, ELECTRONIC WARFARE OFFICER)
ARMAMENT: APPROX 70,000 LBS MIXED ORDNANCE: BOMBS, SMART WEAPONS, MINES AND MISSILES. MODIFIED TO CARRY AIR-LAUNCHED CRUISE MISSILES AND MINIATURE AIR LAUNCHED DECOY

"ENGINEERING ANALYZES HAVE SHOWN THAT THE B-52'S OPERATIONAL LIFESPAN COULD EXTEND BEYOND 2040, AN EXTRAORDINARY ACHIEVEMENT FOR AN AIRCRAFT DESIGN THAT PREDATES THE KOREAN WAR"

The B-52 is still an active part of the US nuclear triad along with submarines and ballistic missiles

Left: A B-52H refuels over Afghanistan. Airborne refueling gives the B-52 an almost limitless global reach. It will only land if there are oil or engine problems

Crews of the B-52 would adorn their aircraft with symbols of achievements such as the number of missions flown

ARMAMENT

B-52s were originally designed to exclusively carry nuclear bombs, which was seen as the primary role. However, the plane can also carry 12 Advanced Cruise Missiles, 20 Air Launched Cruise Missiles or eight standard nuclear bombs. It was not until the F Model that a modification was made to carry additional weapons. A 'Big Belly' modification can pack in a 500-pound bomb along with additional explosives on the wings totaling a weight of 60,000 pounds. This figure needs to be tripled as B-52s always travel in groups of three, usually flying at 40,000 feet to avoid detection.

"THE PLANE IS CAPABLE OF CARRYING 12 ADVANCED CRUISE MISSILES, 20 AIR LAUNCHED CRUISE MISSILES OR EIGHT NUCLEAR BOMBS"

Nuclear destruction was available literally at the flick of a button in the B-52

Below: An AGM-129 ACM. It was the US Air Force's most advanced air-launched nuclear missile until it was decommissioned in 2012

A B-52H displaying the variety of weapons it is capable of carrying, from cluster bombs to harpoons

The 'Special Weapons' on a B-52 are a grim collection of destructive power

Below: The 'Special Weapons' (center top) are controlled from the navigation suite under the cockpit

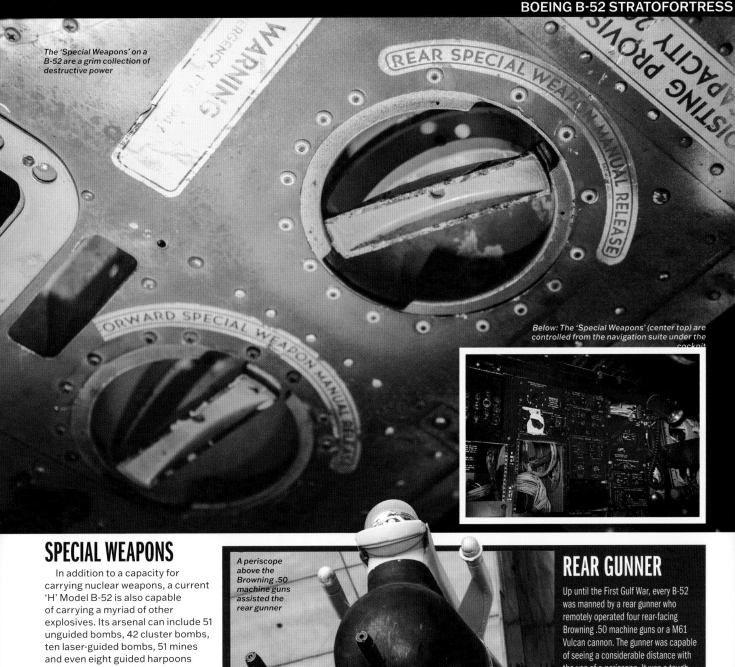

SPECIAL WEAPONS

In addition to a capacity for carrying nuclear weapons, a current 'H' Model B-52 is also capable of carrying a myriad of other explosives. Its arsenal can include 51 unguided bombs, 42 cluster bombs, ten laser-guided bombs, 51 mines and even eight guided harpoons to be used against ships. Perhaps most notoriously, B-52s dropped napalm bombs and incendiaries as a defoliant during the Vietnam War. A single bomb could destroy areas up to 2,500 square yards and the bombers were largely responsible for dropping 8 million tonnes of napalm over Vietnam between 1965-73.

Napalm bombs explode on Vietcong structures. Many B-52s were involved in dropping millions of tons of napalm during the Vietnam War

A periscope above the Browning .50 machine guns assisted the rear gunner

REAR GUNNER

Up until the First Gulf War, every B-52 was manned by a rear gunner who remotely operated four rear-facing Browning .50 machine guns or a M61 Vulcan cannon. The gunner was capable of seeing a considerable distance with the use of a periscope. It was a tough, lonely job, as the aircraft could be airborne for over 24 hours. Unlike his colleagues in the front of the plane, there was no place for the gunner to lie down and sleep. The only way the other crew members could communicate with the gunner was via an interphone. The turbulence could be so bad in the rear, that gunners often suffered from concussion.

"IT WAS A TOUGH, LONELY JOB, AS THE AIRCRAFT COULD BE AIRBORNE FOR OVER 24 HOURS"

The instrumental panel of the B-52 has changed little since the 1950s

COCKPIT

This cockpit dates from 1957 but modern B-52s look almost the same. The only difference between then and now is the use of infrared cameras and low-light televisions. The instrument panel works from the top down. At the top are readings of oil pressure for each engine. In the center are dials for measuring the percentage of the plane's revolutions per minute (rpm) – a B-52 operates at an average of 160,000 rpm. Below this is the exhaust gas temperature, a thermal coupling that measures how hot the air in the plane's rear is. Finally, at the bottom are the readings for fuel flow, which in a B-52 can measure 1,500 pounds per hour.

Right: Dials include readings for pressure, speed, fuel flow, altitude and bearings

A B-52H taking off. To give the engines enough thrust the aircraft needs a runway that is at least 10,000 feet long

"SOME MECHANICS WOULD ONLY ALLOW THREE FORD ENGINES PER AIRCRAFT BECAUSE THEY HAD A REPUTATION FOR BEING UNRELIABLE"

Right: B-52s have eight engines, providing 136,000 lbs of thrust to get 450,000 lbs of aircraft off the ground

POWERPLANT

B-52s were produced on a wartime footing and sometimes employed unconventional contractors to build the engines. For instance, Ford Motor Company made this plane's engines. Ford produced numerous plants for the B-52 but many in the Air Force disliked them. Some mechanics would only allow three Ford engines per aircraft because they had a reputation for being unreliable. Pratt & Witney engines now power modern B-52s.

AMERICAN AIR MUSEUM RESTORATION PROJECT

THE IMPERIAL WAR MUSEUM DUXFORD HAS UNDERTAKEN A MAJOR RESTORATION PROJECT TO PRESERVE OVER A CENTURY'S WORTH OF AMERICAN MILITARY AIRCRAFT. SECTION HEAD, CHRIS KNAPP TELLS US MORE

"The driving force for the project initially was that a lot of these aircraft had been suspended for 17 years and whilst we can inspect the suspensions manually, which we do, we cannot open up the aircraft to inspect the airframe itself. It's still a mechanical object, even though it's a museum piece, and some of them are over 100 years old so we had to get them all down to inspect them. We couldn't find any information anywhere of other museums that had taken aircraft down and inspected them.
"My colleagues in Exhibitions and Displays said that they would re-configure the whole setup and redo everything with new displays. The glass wall had to come down and we had five weeks to get everything out, three months to inspect everything and then five weeks to get it back in. The F-111 and the A-10 were in the original paint that they flew in when they arrived here so we would did a lot to preserve that. The B-52 stood outside for a long time when it first came. The paint had deteriorated so we had to remove it, do some repairs to the corrosion and repaint it. We're careful on whatever we're working with.
"Every project has to stand or fall on its own merit but our primary aim is to preserve the history as much as possible. An object soaks up history; if you handle it you will lose history, the more you handle it the more history you lose. We're in the business of preserving history. A highlight is definitely the B-52. I can tell you the theory of flight but it still amazes me that it gets in the air. In the museum as a whole I have a soft spot for the Westland Wessex and the Sea King because I worked on both of those in service."

"WE'RE IN THE BUSINESS OF PRESERVING HISTORY"

The B-52 forms the centerpiece of the museum

IWM Duxford has a wide array of American military aircraft

F-4 PHANTOM II

One of the most iconic fighter planes ever, the F-4 Phantom II set 15 world records during its lifetime

The F-4 was one of the most technologically advanced fighter-interceptors of its generation. Breaking numerous records – highest altitude flight, fastest flight speed and fastest zoom climb to name but a few – and introducing advanced new construction materials and aviation features, the jet ruled the skies from 1960 up until the end of the Seventies.

The Phantom was powered by a pair of General Electric J79 axial compressor turbojets, which could deliver a whopping 17,845 pounds-force of thrust in afterburner. This, along with its super-strong titanium airframe, granted the aircraft a lift-to-drag ratio of 8.58, a thrust-to-weight ratio of 0.86 and a rate of climb north of 689 feet per second. That extreme amount of power also afforded it a top speed of 1,485 miles per hour.

As a fighter-interceptor, the F-4 was equipped with nine external hardpoints. Air-to-air AIM-9 Sidewinders, air-to-ground AGM-65 Mavericks and anti-ship GBU-15s, as well as a Vulcan six-barreled Gatling cannon, were but a small selection of the heavy-duty weaponry available. In addition, it was also specified to carry a range of nuclear armaments.

Perhaps the biggest innovation delivered by the F-4 Phantom II, however, was the adoption of a pulse-Doppler radar. Still in use today, this is a four-dimensional radar system that's capable of detecting a target's 3D position and its radial velocity. It does this by transmitting short bursts of radio waves (rather than a continuous wave), which after being partially bounced back by the airborne object, are received and decoded by a signal processor, which discerns its location and flight path through the principles of the Doppler effect.

ANATOMY OF AN F-4E PHANTOM II

CHECK OUT THE TECH THAT MADE THE PHANTOM SUCH A RECORD-BREAKING FIGHTER JET

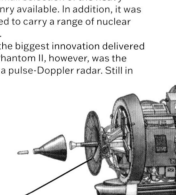

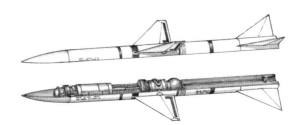

RADAR
One of the Phantom's biggest innovations was its pulse-Doppler radar installed in its nose. This type of radar transmits short pulses of radio waves to determine an object's position and movement

"PERHAPS THE BIGGEST INNOVATION DELIVERED BY THE F-4 PHANTOM II WAS THE ADOPTION OF THE PULSE-DOPPLER RADAR, A FOUR-DIMENSIONAL SYSTEM STILL IN USE TODAY"

A South Korean F-4E patrols the skies, armed with an AGM-65 Maverick missile

Nine external hardpoints could be installed offering an arsenal of heavy firing power

AIRFRAME
The Phantom's airframe was forged heavily from titanium, granting it the strength, durability and heat resistance necessary to perform maneuvers at immense speeds

POWERPLANT
The F-4E was equipped with two GE J79-GE-17A axial compressor turbojets. These delivered a dry thrust of 11,905lbf and 17,845lbf with afterburner engaged

WING
Leading edge slats on both wings greatly improved high angle of attack maneuverability. This enhanced its handling at slow to medium speeds

ARMAMENTS
Up to 18,650lb of weapons on nine hardpoints could be carried. These included laser-guided bombs, rocket pods and heat-seeking missiles

F-4E PHANTOM II
CREW 2
LENGTH 63FT
WINGSPAN 38FT
HEIGHT 16.4FT
POWERPLANT 2X GENERAL ELECTRIC J79-GE-17A TURBOJETS
MAX THRUST 17,845LBF
MAX SPEED 1,485MPH
MAX ALTITUDE 60,000FT

5 Facts about F-4 PHANTOM II

SPOOKY
The Phantom's emblem was a whimsical cartoon ghost referred to as 'The Spook' by pilots. It was designed by McDonnell Douglas technical artist Anthony Wong.

NICKNAMES
The Phantom acquired a number of nicknames during its long career including the Rhino, Flying Anvil, Flying Footlocker, Lead Sled and the St Louis Slugger.

EXPORT
The Phantom was not only used in North America but also in many other national militaries around the world, being exported to Greece, Germany and Iran to name just a few countries.

ANGELS
The F-4J Phantom II variant also saw plenty of non-military action. For instance, it was flown by the US aerobatic display team, the Blue Angels, from 1969 through to 1974.

OBSOLETE
The F-4 Phantom II was eventually superseded by a brace of newer fighter jets manufactured from the Eighties onwards. These included F-14 Tomcats and F/A-18 Hornets.

A Vulcan takes off at Farnborough International Airshow, England

DELTA WING
The Vulcan's revolutionary delta wing plan allowed the engines, undercarriage, fuel tanks and payload to be enclosed within a low-drag profile. This granted the Vulcan great high speed and altitude performance

ELECTRONICS
The Vulcan's electronics included a terrain following radar (TFR), navigation and bombing system (NBS) and H2S radar with nose-mounted scanner. A tail-mounted warning radar also helped to spot enemy aircraft and missiles

PAYLOAD
The Vulcan could carry 1,000lb conventional bombs, a gravity-guided, 10,000lb nuclear bomb or a stand-off nuclear missile. A small number were also installed with Skybolt missiles

AVRO VULCAN

The world's first delta-winged bomber, the Avro Vulcan was an aerial titan, capable of delivering a 4,536kg nuclear bomb to any hostile target within a huge radius

Born in the aftermath of World War II – where despite years of conventional warfare, the war was won in the east with the simple dropping of two atomic bombs on Hiroshima and Nagasaki – the Avro Vulcan was designed to be Britain's first line of atomic offence in future conflicts. A new era of modern warfare was emerging from the flames and dust that had consumed Europe, Africa, Russia, Japan and others. No longer would wars be fought and won by armies – they were to be prevented through the power of splitting the atom. The Vulcan was conceptualized

as a high-altitude, high-speed, strategic bomber, capable of delivering a single 10,000lb nuclear weapon to any target within a distance of 1,725 mi. To achieve this demanding brief, the aircraft needed to feature an innovative aerodynamic structure, as conventional aircraft of the day were unsuitable. Further, as the nuclear weapon itself had yet to be invented, the aircraft would have to be developed in partnership with it, adjusting its plans accordingly.

Upon completion of the Vulcan prototype, it featured a revolutionary delta wing planform

– a triangular wing layout – that granted phenomenal lift and airframe maneuverability. The planform also allowed the jet to fly at high subsonic and transonic speeds with ease and granted it a high angle of attack and stall angle. These features also meant that it was perfectly stable when cruising at low speeds – something normal wings on high-speed aircraft were unable to achieve safely and consistently. In addition, its sleek aerodynamic profile – despite its large size – gave the Vulcan a small radar cross-section, providing a decent level of stealth for the time. Four colossal Bristol Olympus axial-flow

ANATOMY OF THE VULCAN

The Bristol Olympus axial-flow turbojet engines on the Vulcan provide 11,000lb of thrust

AVRO VULCAN B.1

CREW 5

LENGTH 97FT 1IN

WINGSPAN 99FT 5IN

HEIGHT 26FT 6IN

WEIGHT 83,573LB

POWERPLANT 4 X BRISTOL OLYMPUS (11,000LBF EACH)

MAX SPEED 697MPH

MAX RANGE 2,607MI

MAX ALTITUDE 55,000FT

THRUST/WEIGHT RATIO 0.31

ARMAMENT 21 X 1,000LB BOMBS, 1 X 400-KILOTON NUCLEAR BOMB, 1X 1.1-MEGATON NUCLEAR MISSILE

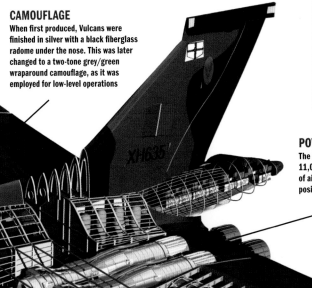

CAMOUFLAGE
When first produced, Vulcans were finished in silver with a black fiberglass radome under the nose. This was later changed to a two-tone grey/green wraparound camouflage, as it was employed for low-level operations

POWERPLANT
The Vulcan's four Bristol Olympus engines delivered 11,000lb of thrust each, and were fed large quantities of air by specially designed letterbox-style inlets positioned at the wings' nearside leading edge

STEALTH
Despite its large size, the Vulcan actually had a small radar cross-section, thanks to its shortened fuselage and swept delta wing plan. In fact, when flying at certain angles that hid its tail fin, it would vanish from radar completely

"THE VULCAN WAS CONCEPTUALISED AS A HIGH-SPEED, STRATEGIC BOMBER CAPABLE OF DELIVERING A NUCLEAR WEAPON"

LETTERBOX

Thanks to the Vulcan's revolutionary delta wing planform, its four Bristol Olympus engines could be enclosed with a low drag shape close to the fuselage to maximize aerodynamic performance at speed. Engines were positioned in pairs and fed by two large letterbox-style air inlets in the wing root leading edge. This ensured that the axial flow turbojets got the right amount of air to operate, with maximum power when needed.

turbojet engines, each capable of delivering 11,000lb of thrust, powered the Vulcan. The engines were paired and buried in the delta wings close to the fuselage, and were fed with air through two large letterbox-style inlets in the wing root leading edge. The positioning of the engines and short fuselage allowed a larger space to be reserved for internal equipment and payload. At full power, the Vulcan could hit a top speed of 697mph, just shy of Mach 1, and could cruise at 567mph/ Mach 0.86.

Partnering the Vulcan's revolutionary design was a comprehensive suite of avionics and electronic systems. Navigation and bombing was handled by an H2S radar with nose-mounted scanner, the first ever airborne, ground-scanning radar system. This allowed the Vulcan's crew to identify and engage targets in night or poor-weather conditions. In addition, a Red Steer tail-warning radar allowed the jet's Air Electronics Operator to quickly spot enemy fighter aircraft and launch chaff and flares accordingly to negate missile attacks. In the second edition of the aircraft, the Vulcan was also outfitted with an AC electrical system, flight refueling probe, autopilot system and electronic counter measure (ECM) suite.

Both the Vulcan's design and advanced technology worked together in order to aid its ability to deliver munitions to enemy targets.

Across its life span, the Vulcan was armed with a variety of nuclear and conventional weapons, ranging from standard free-fall bombs, through nuclear bombs and onto standoff nuclear missiles. Luckily, despite its huge arsenal, the Vulcan was never called upon to go nuclear. Instead it only saw one combat operation (Operation Black Buck) in the Falklands War, dropping conventional bombs on Port Stanley Airport, Falkland Islands.

Despite lack of actual combat missions, the Avro Vulcan is nevertheless seen as a remarkable engineering achievement. It is considered by military historians to be a piece of technology central to nuclear deterrence throughout the 20th century.

F-86 SABRE

Considered the foremost military aircraft of the Fifties, the F-86 Sabre was a highly versatile fighter jet as fast as it was lethal

The F-86 Sabre was a single-seat fighter jet built by North American Aviation (now part of Boeing) in the late-Forties. The aircraft – the first western jet ever to feature swept wings, as well as one of the first aircraft in the world to be capable of breaking the sound barrier in a dive – saw military action throughout the Korean War as well as the Cold War.

Built initially to combat the Russian MiG-15, the Sabre was geared towards flight superiority roles, dispatched to undertake furious high-speed dogfights. Though inferior to the Russian jet in terms of lightness and weaponry, the reduced transonic drag delivered by the swept wings – combined with its streamlined fuselage and advanced electronics – granted it far superior handling. This ability to outmaneuver the MiG-15 soon saw it establish supremacy in combat.

Despite possessing an overall armament inferiority to its rivals, the Sabre was one of the first military jets capable of firing guided air-to-air missiles and later variants, such as the F-86E, were additionally fitted with radar and targeting systems that were revolutionary for the time. These factors, along with its high service ceiling (ie maximum altitude) and its generous range of around 1,000 miles, therefore enabled it to intercept any enemy aircraft with ease.

However, today the Sabre is most known for its world record-breaking performances, with variants of the jet setting five official speed records over a six-year period in the Forties and Fifties. Indeed, the F-86D made history in 1952 by not just setting the overall world speed record (698 miles per hour), but then bettering it by an additional 17 miles per hour the following year.

Today there are no F-86s remaining in service in national militaries, but due to their iconic status and reliable handling, many do remain in operation in the civilian sphere, with around 50 privately owned jets registered in the US alone.

ON BOARD THE F-86E

EXPLORE THE ADVANCED ENGINEERING THAT MAKES THE SABRE SUCH A FORMIDABLE FIGHTER JET…

FUSELAGE
A tapered conical fuselage is installed with a nose cone air inlet. Air is ducted under the cockpit and delivered to the J47 engine before being expelled at the rear via a nozzle

WING
Both wings and tail are swept back, with the former fitted with electrically operated flaps and automatic leading-edge slats. The swept wings lend it excellent agility in dogfights

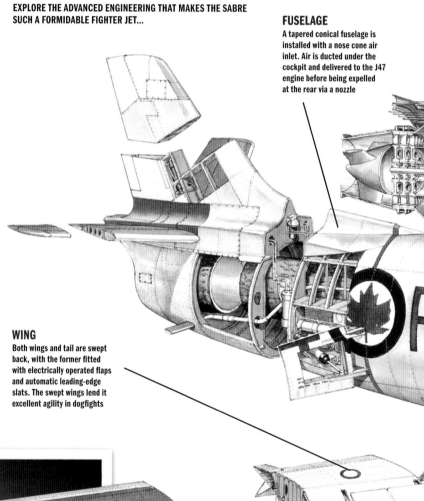

Although built in North America at least 20 other countries used Sabres in their air forces, including Japan, Spain and the UK

"THE F-86 SABRE WAS ONE OF THE FIRST MILITARY JETS CAPABLE OF FIRING GUIDED AIR-TO-AIR MISSILES"

F-86E SABRE

LENGTH 37FT
WINGSPAN 37FT
HEIGHT 14FT
MAX SPEED 650 MPH
RANGE 1,001MI
MAX ALTITUDE 45,000FT
COMBAT WEIGHT 6,350 TONS (14,000LB)

WHO WAS HIGH FLYER JACQUELINE COCHRAN?

Born in 1906, Jacqueline Cochran was a pioneering American aviator and one of the most gifted pilots of her generation. This skill in the air eventually led her to become the first woman in the world to officially break the sound barrier – a truly amazing achievement which she performed in a custom-built, one-off F-86 Sabre.

The record was broken on 18 May 1953 at Rogers Dry Lake in California. In her F-86, Cochran racked up an average speed of 652 miles per hour, breaking the sound barrier with fellow famous pilot Chuck Yeager as her wingman. Cochran would also go on to become the very first woman in history to take off from an aircraft carrier as well as to reach Mach 2.

ENGINE

The F-86E uses a GE J47-13 turbojet engine capable of outputting 5,200lbf of thrust. This raw power grants it a top horizontal speed of about 650mph

COCKPIT

The F-86E is fitted with a small bubble canopy cockpit that covers a single-seat cabin. The cockpit is in a very forward position, tucked just behind the nose cone

ELECTRONICS

An A-1CM gun sight in partnership with an AN/APG-30 radar system makes the F-86E one of the most technologically advanced jets of its time. The radar can quickly work out the range to potential targets

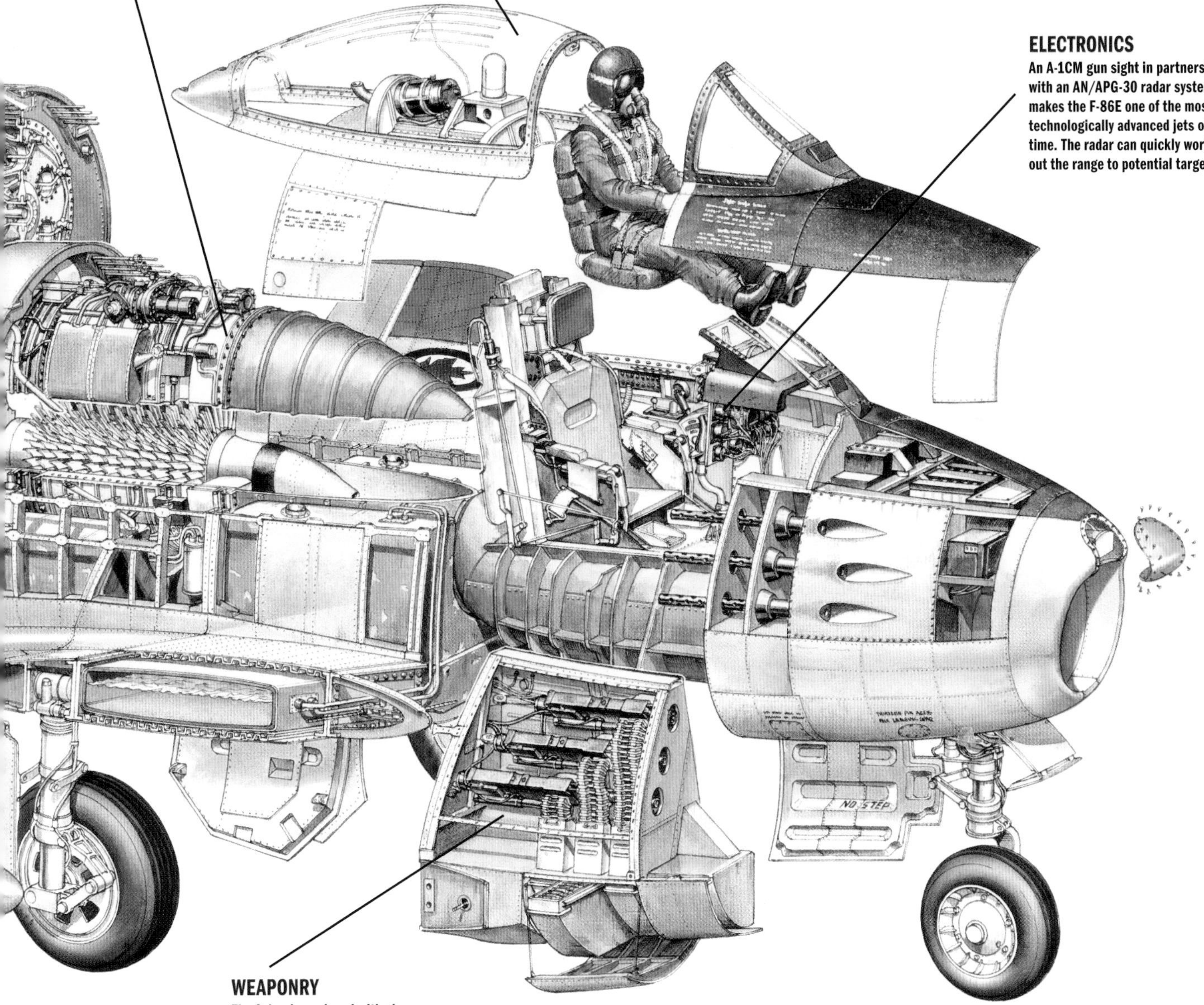

WEAPONRY

The Sabre is equipped with six .50-caliber (12.7mm) M2 Browning machine guns and 16 127mm (5in) HVAR rockets, as well as a variety of freefall bombs and unguided missiles

WESTLAND WESSEX

A versatile helicopter of the Cold War era, the Wessex served with both the Royal Navy and Royal Air Force during its long history

WESTLAND WESSEX

MANUFACTURER: WESTLAND AIRCRAFT
ROLE: ANTI-SUBMARINE; UTILITY
MAXIMUM SPEED: 132MPH
MAXIMUM RANGE: 310MI
POWER: SINGLE NAPIER GAZELLE OR DUAL DE HAVILLAND GNOME GAS TURBINE ENGINES
ARMAMENT: ANTI-SUBMARINE DEPTH CHARGES OR TORPEDOES; 2 PINTLE-MOUNTED 7.62MM MACHINE GUNS; NORD ANTI-TANK MISSILES (VARIANT DEPENDENT)
CREW: 2

"THE WESSEX BECAME THE WORLD'S FIRST HELICOPTER EQUIPPED WITH A GAS TURBINE TO ENTER SERVICE IN LARGE NUMBERS"

During the mid-1950s, the Royal Navy's search for a helicopter capable of performing anti-submarine service, with potential for expanded roles, brought the Sikorsky S-58 to the forefront. Originally developed for the US Navy with the military designation of H-34, the helicopter entered US service in 1954. By 1956, Westland Aircraft, which became Westland Helicopters in 1961, had obtained a license to manufacture it. The first pre-production Wessex helicopter flew in the first half of 1958.

Originally the H-34 was a piston-engined turboshaft helicopter, however, Westland modified the airframe to accommodate a gas turbine powerplant. The Wessex became the world's first helicopter equipped with a gas turbine to enter service in large numbers. Its turbine system originally consisted of a single Napier Gazelle engine, which was followed by the introduction of twin de Havilland Gnome engines. Metal rotor blades were also strengthened to absorb heavier combat damage and remain operational.

The Wessex was subsequently adapted for service with the Royal Air Force, proving adept in several roles. These included search and rescue, cargo transportation and Special Operations troop deployment, as variants were developed for each function. Regarding its initial purpose, the Wessex could not comprehensively conduct each element of anti-submarine warfare since the required equipment and armament would exceed its optimal weight. It was fitted either with sonar hunting and tracking apparatus or armed with weaponry to deal with an identified threat. While the Wessex continued to serve in multiple capacities, the Royal Navy subsequently adopted the Westland Sea King for anti-submarine patrol duties.

A Westland Wessex of the RAF hovers during a mission. The RAF adopted the Wessex in 1962 with a caveat that its airframe accommodate twin gas turbine engines

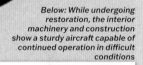

Below: On this Royal Navy-owned Wessex the famed national roundel insignia partially visible at the lower right reveals the helicopter's sturdy construction

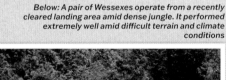

Below: While undergoing restoration, the interior machinery and construction show a sturdy aircraft capable of continued operation in difficult conditions

Below: A pair of Wessexes operate from a recently cleared landing area amid dense jungle. It performed extremely well amid difficult terrain and climate conditions

ENGINES

Two engines powered the Royal Navy and Royal Air Force Wessex variants. A single Napier Gazelle gas turbine powerplant generating 1,650 horsepower drove the Royal Navy Wessex HAS 1 and HAS 3 anti-submarine models. Developed by D Napier & Son, the Gnome entered production in the mid-1950s and was later built under a joint venture with Rolls-Royce.

The RAF required twin powerplants – using dual de Havilland Gnome gas turbine engines, producing 1,550 horsepower in their variants. A license-built version of the General Electric T-58 engine that entered production in 1958, the Gnome was later built by Bristol Siddeley and Rolls-Royce.

Below: Removable panels allowed mechanics easy access to the interior of the Westland Wessex. An engine mount, circuitry, and other equipment are visible in these photos

"THE RAF REQUIRED TWIN POWERPLANTS – USING DUAL DE HAVILLAND GNOME GAS TURBINE ENGINES, PRODUCING 1,550 HORSEPOWER"

The Napier Gazelle gas turbine engine was the single powerplant of the Royal Navy Westland Wessex helicopters

On the deck of a Royal Navy warship, combat ready troops rush to board a Westland Wessex helicopter. The Wessex performed well in the Falklands War of 1982, delivering troops and supplies to combat zones

"RAF HELICOPTERS, SUCH AS THE HC 2, CARRIED UP TO 16 COMBAT-READY TROOPS AND MOUNTED BROWNING MACHINE GUNS FOR PERIMETER SECURITY AND STRAFING"

Right: Soldiers board a Royal Navy Westland Wessex that is preparing for takeoff during training operations. Note the Union Jack painted on the nose of the helicopter

ARMAMENT

The naval HAS 1 was armed with torpedoes or depth charges to engage in the attack phase of anti-submarine warfare, while RAF helicopters, such as the HC 2, carried up to 16 combat-ready troops and mounted Browning machine guns for perimeter security and strafing. Ground attack versions mounted machine guns and up to four French-designed Nord SS-11 anti-tank missiles. The Royal Navy's HU 5 carried 16 Royal Marines along with up to four Browning machine guns, rocket launchers, torpedoes or Nord anti-tank or air-to-ground missiles.

Museum, Weston-super-Mare.
For more information visit:
www.helicoptermuseum.co.uk

"THE WESTLAND WESSEX COCKPIT OFFERED PILOT AND CO-PILOT GOOD VISIBILITY AND A FORWARD CONSOLE WITH STANDARD INSTRUMENTATION"

Central to the forward console of the Westland Wessex cockpit was the attitude indicator, giving the pilot his position relative to an artificial horizon, Numerous gauges are situated around the space

COCKPIT

The Westland Wessex cockpit offered pilot and co-pilot good visibility and a forward console with standard instrumentation. In the center, the attitude indicator gave the pilot his orientation relative to an artificial horizon. The altimeter and RPM gauge were located at the upper-right above the vertical speed indicator and instrument landing system indicator.

The compass was situated directly below the attitude indicator, while the airspeed indicator and torquemeter were at the upper left with the trim release switch just below. The cyclic stick was positioned centrally to the pilot's seat with the collective lever, controlling blade pitch, at lower left.

The collective lever at left controlled blade pitch and was critical to the pilot's ability to maintain control of the aircraft. The cyclic stick is centered to the pilot's seat

Royal Navy Westland Wessex helicopters of 707 Naval Air Squadron are lined up at an airfield in preparation for takeoff

DESIGN

In the early 1950s, Sikorsky engineers began the development of the S-58 helicopter as a longer and more robust variant of its earlier S-55. Specifically intended for anti-submarine warfare, the S-58 airframe was modified with a tail dragger rear fuselage and landing gear. Its

Wright Cyclone piston engine was nose-mounted with the drive shaft passing through the cockpit. In 1956, Westland procured a single S-58. Alterations were made to accommodate the lighter Napier Gazelle gas turbine engine. Weight redistribution was required, and the Wessex prototype flew within a few months. The RAF began operating the twin-engined Wessex in 1962.

SERVICE HISTORY

Nearly 400 Westland Wessex helicopters in at least a dozen variants were produced for the Royal Navy and RAF from 1958 to 1970. The service life of the Wessex extended until the last were retired from RAF service on the island of Cyprus in 2003. During its military career, the versatile Wessex was involved in anti-submarine, troop carrying and utility operations around the globe.

The helicopter engaged in peacetime humanitarian rescue and relief efforts and joint military exercises, as well as frontline operations during wartime. Initial combat service occurred in the early 1960s during an armed crisis in Indonesia. Wessex helicopters of the Royal Navy and RAF supported ground troops battling guerrilla forces. These aircraft performed cargo and transport missions with payloads up to 1,800 kilograms. The Wessex also patrolled the skies above Northern Ireland during periods of civil unrest. During the 1982 Falklands War, the Wessex delivered

substantial support in utility and combat roles. Nine of the helicopters were destroyed during the war, including six that sank with the container ship Atlantic Conveyer, which was turned into an inferno by two Argentine Exocet anti-ship missiles. Another was lost when an Exocet damaged the destroyer, HMS Glamorgan.

Perhaps the most heroic chapter of the type's wartime service occurred in the Falklands, when the crew of a Wessex nicknamed Humphrey, flying from the destroyer HMS Antrim, rescued numerous Special Forces troops and crewmen of two other Wessexes that had crashed in horrific weather on the Fortuna Glacier during a mission to observe Argentine movements. Humphrey crewmen also spotted the Argentine submarine Santa Fe and led the attack that caused the enemy to abandon ship. Humphrey was aboard Antrim when Argentine fighter jets strafed the vessel. Damage to its fuselage was patched with tape and the durable Wessex continued to operate.

With a service life of more than 40 years, the Westland Wessex helicopter saw action while serving the armed forces of numerous nations

C-130 HERCULES

One of the longest-lasting and most widespread military transport vehicles of all time, the C-130 Hercules remains to this day an aerial behemoth, capable of flying thousands of miles to deploy troops and vehicles alike

The C-130 Hercules is a military transport aircraft famed for its durability and versatility, having been in active service for over 50 years. Since its introduction in December 1957, over 40 models and variants of the Hercules have been produced and are used today by more than 60 nations worldwide.

The aircraft works by delivering a cavernous central fuselage in which the vast cargo bay can carry a plethora of civilians, soldiers, vehicles, equipment, weapons and supplies over huge distances. This makes the Hercules an ideal tool to aid military operations in the 21st-century battlefield, where mission parameters often need to adapt fluidly and at high speed.

Indeed, the sheer lifting power of the C-130 cannot be overstated, with a single plane capable of lifting northwards of 72,753 pounds. To put that in context, that is an ability to lift the equivalent of seven fully grown African elephants or 44 Mini Metros! As a heavy-lifting workhorse, the C-130 has few competitors capable of matching it and, as such, has seen off several contenders that were supposed to replace it (such as the C-5 Galaxy) and even spawned a larger but rarer Super Hercules variant.

All that lift comes courtesy of four Allison T56 turboprop jet engines, each capable of generating 4,590 shaft horsepower. The combined output makes this plane more powerful than 15 Bugatti Veyron Super Sports – the most powerful car on the planet. It also means the Hercules can not just lift more than 72,753 pounds, but it can do so at both high altitude (the C-130 has a service ceiling of 33,000 feet) and at high speed, with a cruise speed of 336 miles per hour. In addition, the titanic turboprops allow the Hercules to climb at a rate of 31 feet per second, a fact that allows it to quickly get airborne and out of range of many anti-aircraft armaments.

Interestingly, despite the US Air Force aiming to instigate a program to produce a replacement for the C-130 in 2014 – for eventual delivery in 2024 – uptake for the program has not been marked. Further, in December 2011, Lockheed Martin – the manufacturer of the Hercules – announced two new variants of the Hercules: the C-130XJ and C-130NG. As such, despite the aircraft being over 60 old, it is unlikely that it will be retiring in the next decade at least.

ANATOMY OF A C-130 HERCULES

WE BREAK DOWN A POPULAR VARIANT OF THIS AERIAL TITAN

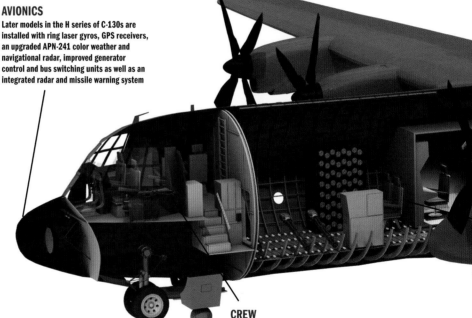

AVIONICS
Later models in the H series of C-130s are installed with ring laser gyros, GPS receivers, an upgraded APN-241 color weather and navigational radar, improved generator control and bus switching units as well as an integrated radar and missile warning system

CREW
Due to its tremendous size and flexible capabilities, the C-130H is manned by five crew members. There are two pilots, a navigator, flight engineer and loadmaster. Due to its large carrying capacity, the loadmaster's role is to determine how to most efficiently load huge and diverse cargo

"THE HERCULES IS AN IDEAL TOOL TO AID MILITARY OPERATIONS IN THE FAST-CHANGING CONTEMPORARY BATTLEFIELD "

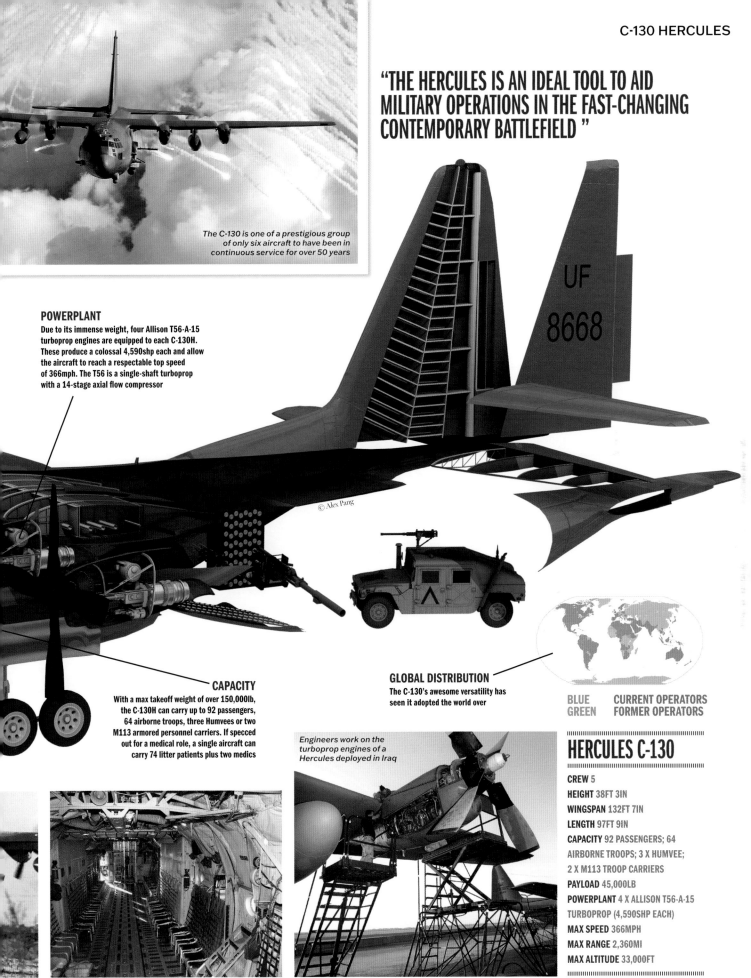

The C-130 is one of a prestigious group of only six aircraft to have been in continuous service for over 50 years

UF 8668

© Alex Pang

POWERPLANT
Due to its immense weight, four Allison T56-A-15 turboprop engines are equipped to each C-130H. These produce a colossal 4,590shp each and allow the aircraft to reach a respectable top speed of 366mph. The T56 is a single-shaft turboprop with a 14-stage axial flow compressor

CAPACITY
With a max takeoff weight of over 150,000lb, the C-130H can carry up to 92 passengers, 64 airborne troops, three Humvees or two M113 armored personnel carriers. If specced out for a medical role, a single aircraft can carry 74 litter patients plus two medics

GLOBAL DISTRIBUTION
The C-130's awesome versatility has seen it adopted the world over

BLUE — CURRENT OPERATORS
GREEN — FORMER OPERATORS

Engineers work on the turboprop engines of a Hercules deployed in Iraq

HERCULES C-130

CREW 5
HEIGHT 38FT 3IN
WINGSPAN 132FT 7IN
LENGTH 97FT 9IN
CAPACITY 92 PASSENGERS; 64 AIRBORNE TROOPS; 3 X HUMVEE; 2 X M113 TROOP CARRIERS
PAYLOAD 45,000LB
POWERPLANT 4 X ALLISON T56-A-15 TURBOPROP (4,590SHP EACH)
MAX SPEED 366MPH
MAX RANGE 2,360MI
MAX ALTITUDE 33,000FT

A-10 THUNDERBOLT II

Why is the A-10 Thunderbolt fighter jet still in use today, and just as popular as it was four decades ago when it first took off?

The A-10 Thunderbolt is a single-seat, close-air support fighter jet that also goes by the names Warthog and Tankbuster. Development for the aircraft began in 1967 and its first flight was in 1972. There are several reasons why the A-10 has proved popular enough to weather 40-plus years of advancing military tech – chief among them its combat versatility and high survival rate.

The A-10 boasts a short takeoff and landing capacity with a range of nearly 800 miles. Commonly used for troop support and ground attacks, it can loiter for long periods at low speeds and altitudes below 985 feet and it's capable of soaking up as much damage as it can dish out. Indeed, the A-10 can take direct hits from armor-piercing and explosive shells, has multiple redundancies for its flight systems and, most incredibly, it can return to base on one engine, one tail stabilizer, one elevator and even having lost half a wing! As a result, it's well known among US Air Force pilots for its 'get home' effectiveness.

Modern A-10s have been upgraded from the original 1972 blueprint, of course. Navigation and targeting systems have been dramatically improved. Pilots can now wear night-vision goggles for low-light ops, plus a host of electronic counter-measures and smart-bomb capacity have been installed.

A-10 THUNDERBOLT II TECH

WE'VE PULLED APART THE WARTHOG TO SEE WHAT MAKES IT SUCH A HARDY AIRCRAFT

FUEL TANKS
The Warthog's four main fuel tanks are self-sealing and lined with fire-retardant foam

COCKPIT
Contains targeting and navigation controls for the pilot, including a heads-up display and secure radio communications

CANOPY
Both the windscreen and the transparent bubble canopy are resistant to small arms fire

LANDING GEAR
Landing gear is hinged at the rear so that if the hydraulic system fails, wind resistance and gravity will fully open and lock them in place

MAIN CANNON
The General Dynamics Avenger 30mm (1.2in) cannon can fire standard, incendiary or even depleted-uranium rounds

An A-10A cruising during Operation Allied Force

"COMMONLY USED FOR TROOP SUPPORT AND GROUND ATTACKS, IT CAN LOITER FOR LONG PERIODS AT LOW ALTITUDES"

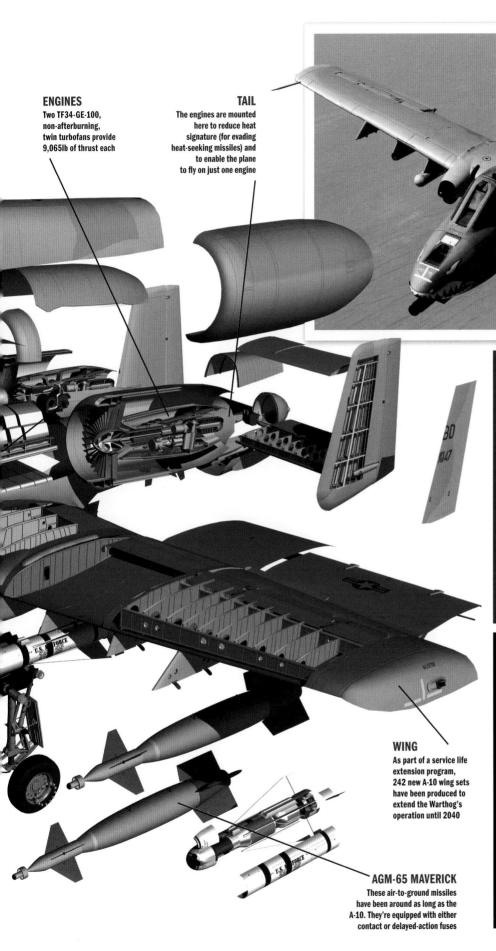

The US Air Force boasts over 360 A-10s in its fleet, operating all around the world, including this one in Afghanistan

ENGINES
Two TF34-GE-100, non-afterburning, twin turbofans provide 9,065lb of thrust each

TAIL
The engines are mounted here to reduce heat signature (for evading heat-seeking missiles) and to enable the plane to fly on just one engine

WING
As part of a service life extension program, 242 new A-10 wing sets have been produced to extend the Warthog's operation until 2040

AGM-65 MAVERICK
These air-to-ground missiles have been around as long as the A-10. They're equipped with either contact or delayed-action fuses

BUILT FOR DEFENCE

The A-10 is robust enough to sustain heavy damage during combat and remain capable of flying away, where other aircraft would be compromised. It's exceptionally well-armored around the cockpit, where the pilot is vulnerable. Sensitive parts of the flight control system, along with the pilot, are shielded by a 'tub' of titanium armor: 1,200 pounds of this super-hard metal is layered in plates up to 1.5 inches thick around the cockpit, based on the likely trajectories of incoming projectiles. It can withstand fire from similar cannons to its own main weapon, as well as large-caliber rounds. A nylon spall shield also protects the pilot from shrapnel and round fragmentation, while the transparent canopy (which can't afford the same level of protection) can still resist ballistics from small arms.

ON THE OFFENSIVE

The A-10 can carry nearly half its weight again in armaments and their associated systems, with an external load of up to 16,005 pounds. It's equipped with 11 pylons along which laser weapon guidance and support systems can be attached, plus ordnance. It's capable of carrying a range of cluster and 500-pound general-purpose bombs, Hydra rockets, plus up to ten Maverick air-to-ground missiles weighing 670 pounds apiece. The latter can destroy a tank in a single hit – however, at a cost of up to $160,000 a pop, a cavalier attitude with the Mavericks is not tolerated. The main weapon is the Avenger 1.2-inch cannon mounted under the nose of the A-10, with a top fire rate of 4,200 rounds a minute and an effective range of over four miles. The cannon can easily disable a main battle tank in the hands of a competent pilot.

© Alex Pang

DASSAULT MIRAGE 2000

A lightweight aircraft boasting diverse multi-role functionality, the Dassault Mirage 2000 epitomizes fourth-generation fighter jets, delivering an excellent high-speed flight profile and a low radar signature

Two Mirage 2000Cs during a Baltic air policing deployment role

INSIDE A MIRAGE 2000C

WE BREAK OPEN THIS CELEBRATED MULTI-ROLE FIGHTER TO SEE WHAT MAKES IT SO VERSATILE

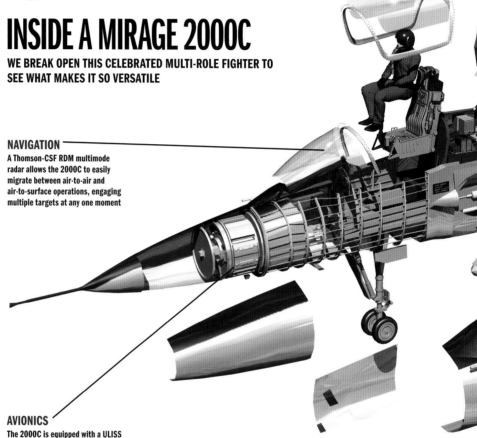

NAVIGATION

A Thomson-CSF RDM multimode radar allows the 2000C to easily migrate between air-to-air and air-to-surface operations, engaging multiple targets at any one moment

AVIONICS

The 2000C is equipped with a ULISS 52 inertial navigation system, TRT radio altimeter, Type 2084 digital flight controller and Sextant Avionique Type 90 air data computer

Despite being overshadowed by more glamorous aircraft over the last 30 years, the Dassault Mirage 2000 series of multi-role fighter jets has quietly delivered excellent functionality and cost efficiency for its operators, which as of 2012, included nations from Europe, through the Middle East and on to Asia. Of course, it is not all über-hyped eco-credentials and safety features that have heightened and maintained the Mirage's popularity among air forces worldwide – but primarily its ability to deliver extreme lethality to air, sea and land targets alike with a whole arsenal of deadly weapons.

We're talking nine hardpoints, two powerful revolving 1.2-inch cannons, multiple Matra rocket pods each capable of launching 18 2.7-inch unguided rockets, two R550 Magic short-range air-to-air missiles, two Super 530 medium-range air-to-air missiles, two Exocet AM-39 anti-ship missiles, two AS-30L, laser-guided air-to-ground missiles and the motherload… the ability to deliver a single ASMP tactical nuclear cruise missile into the heart of any region within a 186-mile range. As mentioned, when you have this vastness and flexibility of payload on offer, maintenance becomes less of an issue, as let a 2000-series out of the hangar and soon there are no targets left to hit.

Complementing this insane level of firepower are equally mind-boggling performance characteristics, something granted by the collaboration of a slick delta-wing planform and explosive SNECMA M53-P2 afterburning turbofan powerplant. The M53-P2 enables the Mirage 2000 to hit a top speed of 1,500 miles per hour and allows it to climb to an altitude of 53,000 feet in a minute. The engine's power – which produces on afterburner a maximum of 22,000 pounds

force of thrust – is enhanced thanks to the 2000's adjustable half-cone air intakes, which provide inclined shocks of air pressure for an incredibly efficient air intake at high speeds.

And it is at these high speeds that the Mirage 2000's delta-wing planform really comes into its own, delivering snake-like agility and fluidity of movement. This works because the triangular rearward sweep angle of the jet's wings vastly lowers the airspeed normal to their leading edges, while simultaneously ensuring the over-wing speed remains less than the speed of sound. This, combined with their inherent large surface area, grants huge lift and minimal wing per unit loading and, as such, super-high airframe maneuverability.

This phenomenal agility is further enhanced

Despite the Mirage 2000 production program ending in 2007, many are still in active service today

"THE DOUBLE-WHAMMY OF AWESOME PERFORMANCE AND INCREDIBLE FIREPOWER ENSURES THAT THE MIRAGE IS STILL BEING USED TODAY"

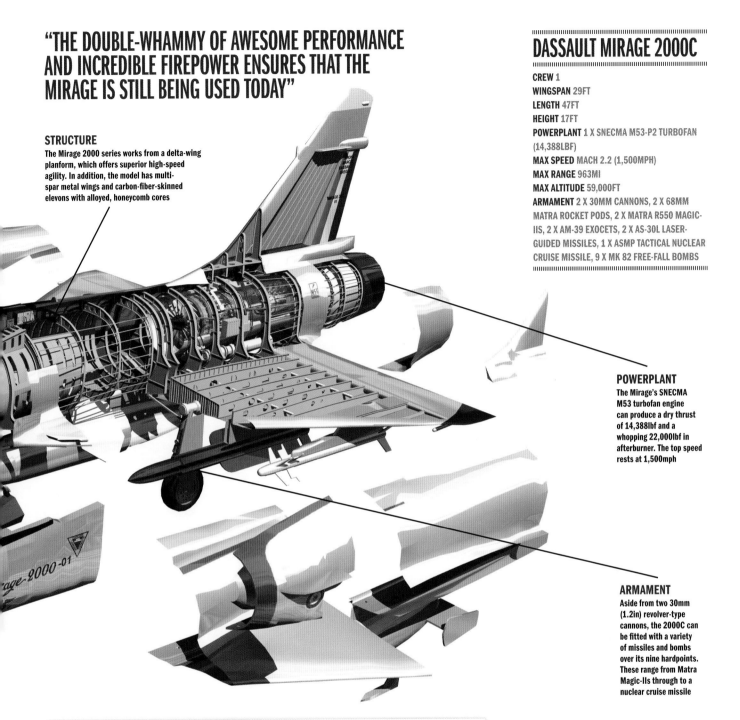

STRUCTURE
The Mirage 2000 series works from a delta-wing planform, which offers superior high-speed agility. In addition, the model has multi-spar metal wings and carbon-fiber-skinned elevons with alloyed, honeycomb cores

DASSAULT MIRAGE 2000C

CREW 1
WINGSPAN 29FT
LENGTH 47FT
HEIGHT 17FT
POWERPLANT 1 X SNECMA M53-P2 TURBOFAN (14,388LBF)
MAX SPEED MACH 2.2 (1,500MPH)
MAX RANGE 963MI
MAX ALTITUDE 59,000FT
ARMAMENT 2 X 30MM CANNONS, 2 X 68MM MATRA ROCKET PODS, 2 X MATRA R550 MAGIC-IIS, 2 X AM-39 EXOCETS, 2 X AS-30L LASER-GUIDED MISSILES, 1 X ASMP TACTICAL NUCLEAR CRUISE MISSILE, 9 X MK 82 FREE-FALL BOMBS

POWERPLANT
The Mirage's SNECMA M53 turbofan engine can produce a dry thrust of 14,388lbf and a whopping 22,000lbf in afterburner. The top speed rests at 1,500mph

ARMAMENT
Aside from two 30mm (1.2in) revolver-type cannons, the 2000C can be fitted with a variety of missiles and bombs over its nine hardpoints. These range from Matra Magic-IIs through to a nuclear cruise missile

A Mirage 2000B variant pre-takeoff. The jet can climb 53,000ft in 60 seconds

by the Mirage being designed with an offset neutral point, which is pushed further forward on the jet than its center of gravity. This means that the aircraft is fundamentally unstable during flight, which though it sounds dangerous, enables the pilot to make tighter, physics-bending moves.

Indeed, the double-whammy of awesome performance and the potential to deal a massive amount of damage when cleared for takeoff is ensuring that, despite the Mirage production program ceasing several years ago, the jet is still being actively used today, representing countries both at home and abroad. A good example of this continued respect for the aircraft's combat abilities can be seen in France's recent deployment of Mirage 2000s in the enforcement of the no-fly zone in Libya in 2011.

SEA HARRIER

Before being retired in 2006, the Sea Harrier dominated the subsonic jet fighter field, changing the dynamics and operation of the strike fighter role forever

The British Aerospace Sea Harrier was the purpose-built naval variant of the Hawker Siddeley Harrier strike fighter, an aircraft that was famed for its vertical take-off and landing (VTOL) and short take-off and vertical landing (STOVL) capabilities. It worked by adopting the revolutionary single-engine thrust vectoring technology of the regular harrier (see 'Degrees of power' boxout) and partnering it with a modified fuselage – in order to allow the installation of the superb Blue Fox radar system – a bubble-style canopy (larger, allowing greater visibility) and a significantly improved arms load out.

These factors, partnered with the aircraft carrier's ability to launch the aircraft from its ski-jump, allowed the Sea Harrier to perform to a high standard at sea, carrying more weight, detecting enemies sooner and taking them down quickly and efficiently. This was demonstrated most vividly during the Falklands War of 1982, when 28 Sea Harriers operating off British aircraft carriers shot down 20 Argentine aircraft in air-to-air combat without suffering a single loss. The Sea Harrier squadron achieved this due to their high maneuverability and tactics while in dogfights – for example, braking/changing direction fast by vectoring their thrust nozzles while in forward flight – as well as their pilots' superior training and early-warning/detection systems.

© John Batchelor / www.johnbatchelor.com

THRUST VECTORING
To achieve VTOL capabilities, the Sea Harrier's engine thrust was directed through four vectoring nozzles, which could rotate through 98.5 degrees from vertically downwards to horizontal

PROTECTION
Due to the testing marine operating conditions, parts of the Sea Harrier were changed to use corrosion-resistant alloys or protective coatings

Second-generation Sea Harriers on board an aircraft carrier in the Persian Gulf

Two Indian Navy Sea Harriers fly alongside a US Navy F/A-18F Super Hornet

"THE SEA HARRIER SQUADRON ACHIEVED THIS DUE TO THEIR HIGH MANEUVERABILITY"

POWERPLANT
The Sea Harrier was fitted with the Rolls-Royce Pegasus 11 turbofan, an engine capable of producing 21,495 pounds of force. This delivered a massive amount of power, which while not taking the jet to supersonic speeds did allow it to lift off vertically, spreading the output over multiple outlets positioned over the aircraft

CREW
The first-generation Sea Harrier FRS1 and second-generation FA2 were both single-seat fighters. However, the T4N and T60 varieties were built with two seats as they were used for land-based pilot conversion training

ELECTRONICS
Equipped according to generation by the Ferranti Blue Fox or Blue Vixen radars respectively, the Sea Harrier carried at the time some of the most advanced military radar systems in the world. It is suggested by military historians that the Blue Fox radar was one of the key reasons why the Sea Harrier performed so successfully in the Falklands War

SEA HARRIER FA2

CREW 1
LENGTH 47FT
WINGSPAN 25FT
HEIGHT 12FT
MAX TAKE-OFF WEIGHT 26,235LB
POWERPLANT 1 X ROLLS-ROYCE PEGASUS TURBOFAN (21,500LBF)
MAX SPEED 735MPH
COMBAT RADIUS 621MI
MAX RANGE 50MI
MAX SERVICE CEILING 9.9MI
GUNS 2 X 30MM ADEN CANNON PODS (100 ROUNDS PER CANNON)
ROCKETS 72 SNEB 68MM ROCKETS
MISSILES AIM-9 SIDEWINDER, AIM-120 AMRAAM, R550 MAGIC, ALARM ANTI-RADIATION MISSILE, MARTEL MISSILE, SEA EAGLE ANTI-SHIP MISSILE
COST $18 MILLION

Some Harriers were fitted with the AIM-120 AMRAAM missile

ARMAMENT
As a strike fighter the Sea Harrier was equipped with a broad arsenal, ranging from conventional, unguided iron bombs – including WE.177 nuclear options – to rockets and laser-guided missiles such as the AIM-9 Sidewinder. The second generation FA2 was famously equipped with deadly AIM-120 AMRAAM air-to-air, fire and forget missiles

DEGREES OF POWER
GIVING THE SEA HARRIER LIFT OFF

The real showpiece and reason for the lengthy success of the Sea Harrier was its utilization of the its revolutionary Pegasus engine partnered with thrust vectoring nozzles. These nozzles could be rotated by the pilot through a 98.5 degree arc, from the conventional aft (horizontal) positioning as standard on aircraft, to straight down, allowing it to take off and land vertically as well as hover, to forward, allowing the Harrier to drift backwards. All nozzles were moved by a series of shafts and chain drives, which insured that they operated in unison (crucial for maintaining stability) and the angle and thrust was determined in-cockpit by the pilot.

This flexibility of control and placement meant that the Sea Harrier was highly maneuverable while in the air and could be landed and launched from almost anywhere.

The Sea Harrier's vectoring nozzle in aft position

002

MIKOYAN MIG-29

Russia's primary fighter jet combines a host of advanced tech to create an agile and deadly aircraft

Often overlooked in the West due to its Soviet Union origins in the Eighties, the Mikoyan MiG-29 is one of the world's most prolific fighter jets, with over 1,600 units in operation around the globe. For perspective, there are just over 300 Eurofighter Typhoons currently in operation, a number that is unlikely to ever exceed the 500 mark.

So why is this Russian plane so successful? For starters, it's great value for money – $29 million, compared to the $104.6 million Typhoon.

The MiG-29 is a fourth-generation fighter jet designed for an air supremacy role, which involves infiltrating and seizing enemy airspace through force. It comes in a range of variants, with both legacy and current production models in operation, and has seen significant combat throughout its 19-year service, including deployment in the Persian Gulf War.

The aircraft is built around an aluminium airframe, which is bolstered with advanced composite materials. This airframe is designed for up to 9g maneuvers, making the jet insanely agile and easy to fly for skilled pilots – hence why it's often used at air shows.

Surrounding the airframe is a sculpted titanium/aluminium alloy fuselage that tapers in from a wide rear to a raised cockpit and elongated nose cone. From the fuselage extends the mid-mounted swept wings, which are installed with leading-edge root extensions.

The MiG-29 is powered by two widely spaced Klimov RD-33 afterburning turbofans that, besides granting a top speed of 1,490 miles per hour, also reduce effective wing loading thanks to their spacing. The engines are fed by an internal fuel system that parses its total reserves down into a series of sub-tanks.

The MiG-29 comes packing a vast arsenal too. Each jet is fitted with seven hardpoints capable of carrying an array of weapons, or external fuel tanks for longer missions.

ANATOMY OF A MIG-29B

THE ESSENTIAL HARDWARE OF THIS RUSSIAN AIR SUPERIORITY FIGHTER REVEALED

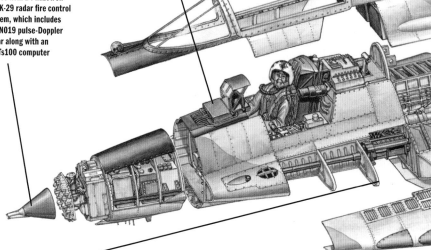

COCKPIT
The MiG-29B's cockpit has a bubble canopy and comes equipped with a conventional center stick, left-hand throttle controls and a heads-up display. Pilots sit in a Zvezda K-36DM ejection seat

SENSORS
The stock MiG-29B comes with a Phazotron RLPK-29 radar fire control system, which includes the N019 pulse-Doppler radar along with an NII Ts100 computer

AIRFRAME
The MiG-29B's airframe is made primarily from aluminium and composite materials. The airframe is stressed for up to 9g maneuvers, making it an extremely agile jet

WEAPONS
The MiG-29B comes with seven hardpoints, each capable of carrying a selection of arms (such as R-73 air-to-air missiles) and bombs. In addition, it carries a single GSh-30-1 30mm (1.2in) cannon

A MiG-29 from the Serbian Air Force takes off

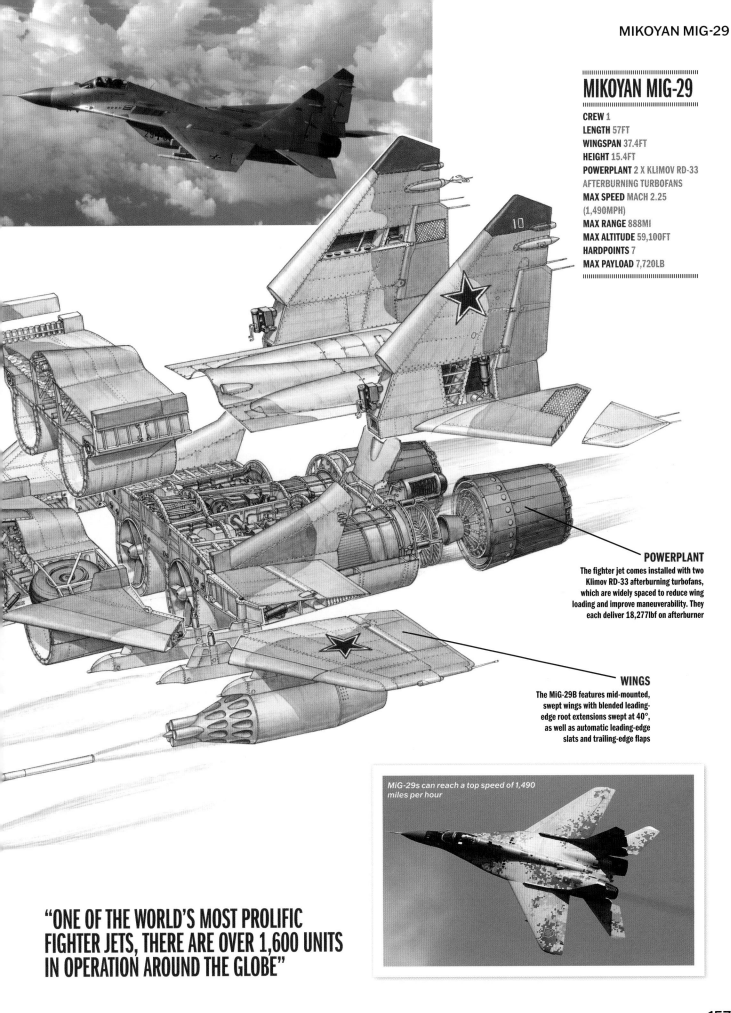

MIKOYAN MIG-29

CREW 1
LENGTH 57FT
WINGSPAN 37.4FT
HEIGHT 15.4FT
POWERPLANT 2 X KLIMOV RD-33 AFTERBURNING TURBOFANS
MAX SPEED MACH 2.25 (1,490MPH)
MAX RANGE 888MI
MAX ALTITUDE 59,100FT
HARDPOINTS 7
MAX PAYLOAD 7,720LB

POWERPLANT
The fighter jet comes installed with two Klimov RD-33 afterburning turbofans, which are widely spaced to reduce wing loading and improve maneuverability. They each deliver 18,277lbf on afterburner

WINGS
The MiG-29B features mid-mounted, swept wings with blended leading-edge root extensions swept at 40°, as well as automatic leading-edge slats and trailing-edge flaps

MiG-29s can reach a top speed of 1,490 miles per hour

"ONE OF THE WORLD'S MOST PROLIFIC FIGHTER JETS, THERE ARE OVER 1,600 UNITS IN OPERATION AROUND THE GLOBE"

STEALTH BOMBER

The B-2 is extraordinary, both in terms of appearance and design

The 'flying wing' shaped Stealth Bomber is a unique aircraft that's designed to make it as invisible as possible. Its shape means there are very few leading edges for radar to reflect from, reducing its signature dramatically. This is further enhanced by the composite materials from which the aircraft is constructed and the coatings on its surface. These are so successful that despite having a 172-foot wingspan, the B-2's radar signature is an astounding 0.1m2.

The B-2's stealth capabilities, and aerodynamic shape, are further enhanced by the fact its engines are buried inside the wing. This means the induction fans at the front of the engines are concealed while the engine exhaust is minimized. As a result, the B-2's thermal signature is kept to the bare minimum, making it harder for thermal sensors to detect the bomber as well as lowering the aircraft's acoustic footprint.

The design also means the B-2 is both highly aerodynamic and fuel efficient. The B-2's maximum range is 6,000 nautical miles and as a result the aircraft has often been used for long-range missions, some lasting 30 hours and in one case, 50. The B-2 is so highly automated that it's possible for a single crew member to fly while the other sleeps, uses the lavatory or prepares a hot meal and this combination of range and versatility has meant the aircraft has been used to research sleep cycles to improve crew performance on long-range missions.

Despite this, the aircraft's success comes with a hefty price tag. Each B-2 costs $737 million and must be kept in a climate-controlled hangar to make sure the stealth materials remain intact. These problems aside though, the Spirit is an astonishing aircraft, even though, chances are, you won't see one unless the pilots want you to.

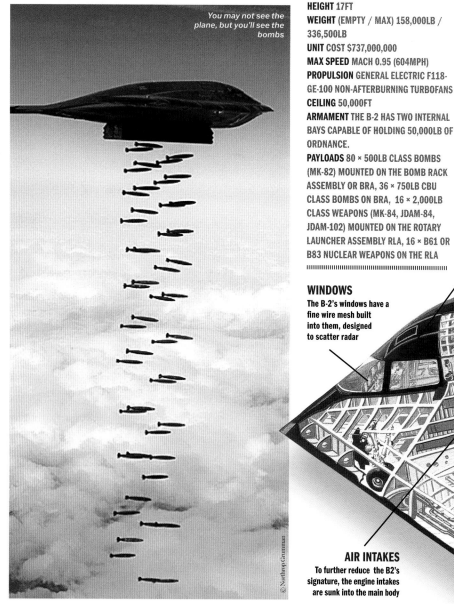

You may not see the plane, but you'll see the bombs

© Northrop Grumman

B-2 SPIRIT

MANUFACTURER: NORTHROP GRUMMAN
YEAR DEPLOYED: 1993
LENGTH 69FT
WINGSPAN 172FT
HEIGHT 17FT
WEIGHT (EMPTY / MAX) 158,000LB / 336,500LB
UNIT COST $737,000,000
MAX SPEED MACH 0.95 (604MPH)
PROPULSION GENERAL ELECTRIC F118-GE-100 NON-AFTERBURNING TURBOFANS
CEILING 50,000FT
ARMAMENT THE B-2 HAS TWO INTERNAL BAYS CAPABLE OF HOLDING 50,000LB OF ORDNANCE.
PAYLOADS 80 × 500LB CLASS BOMBS (MK-82) MOUNTED ON THE BOMB RACK ASSEMBLY OR BRA, 36 × 750LB CBU CLASS BOMBS ON BRA, 16 × 2,000LB CLASS WEAPONS (MK-84, JDAM-84, JDAM-102) MOUNTED ON THE ROTARY LAUNCHER ASSEMBLY RLA, 16 × B61 OR B83 NUCLEAR WEAPONS ON THE RLA

WINDOWS
The B-2's windows have a fine wire mesh built into them, designed to scatter radar

AIR INTAKES
To further reduce the B2's signature, the engine intakes are sunk into the main body

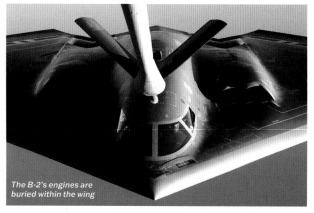

The B-2's engines are buried within the wing

Landings are fine, if the tower spots you coming...

Not one you're likely to find in your I-Spy book...

GHOST WORKS: INSIDE THE SPIRIT

THE B-2 IS AN UNUSUAL COMBINATION OF COMPLEXITY AND ELEGANCE, THE ENTIRE AIRFRAME BUILT AROUND THE CONCEPT OF STEALTH AND FOCUSED ON MAKING THE AIRCRAFT AS HARD TO DETECT AS POSSIBLE

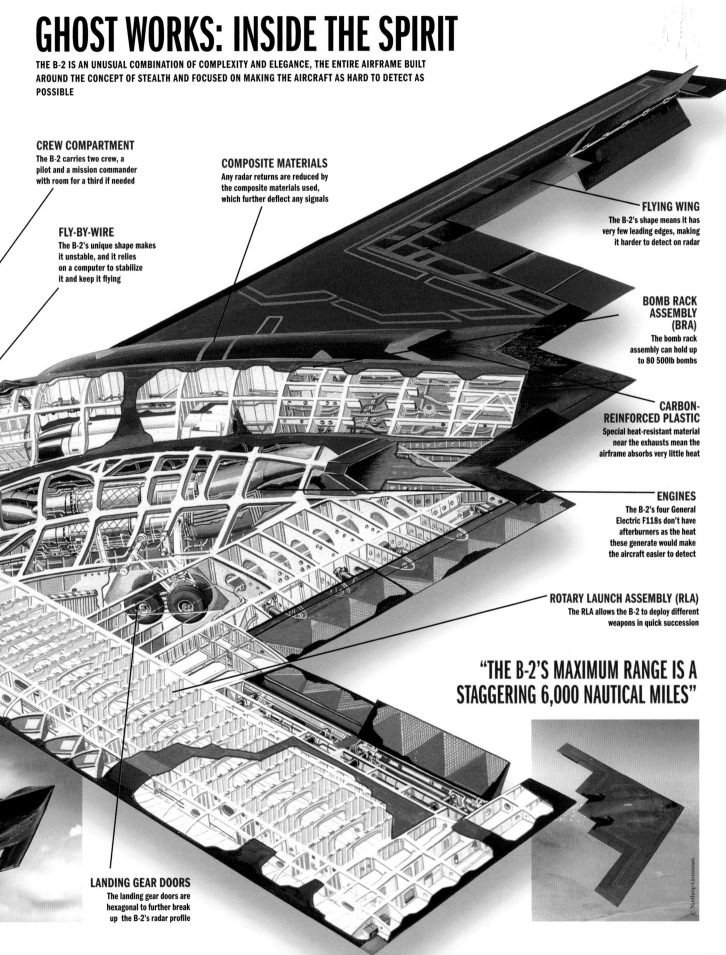

CREW COMPARTMENT
The B-2 carries two crew, a pilot and a mission commander with room for a third if needed

COMPOSITE MATERIALS
Any radar returns are reduced by the composite materials used, which further deflect any signals

FLY-BY-WIRE
The B-2's unique shape makes it unstable, and it relies on a computer to stabilize it and keep it flying

FLYING WING
The B-2's shape means it has very few leading edges, making it harder to detect on radar

BOMB RACK ASSEMBLY (BRA)
The bomb rack assembly can hold up to 80 500lb bombs

CARBON-REINFORCED PLASTIC
Special heat-resistant material near the exhausts mean the airframe absorbs very little heat

ENGINES
The B-2's four General Electric F118s don't have afterburners as the heat these generate would make the aircraft easier to detect

ROTARY LAUNCH ASSEMBLY (RLA)
The RLA allows the B-2 to deploy different weapons in quick succession

"THE B-2'S MAXIMUM RANGE IS A STAGGERING 6,000 NAUTICAL MILES"

LANDING GEAR DOORS
The landing gear doors are hexagonal to further break up the B-2's radar profile

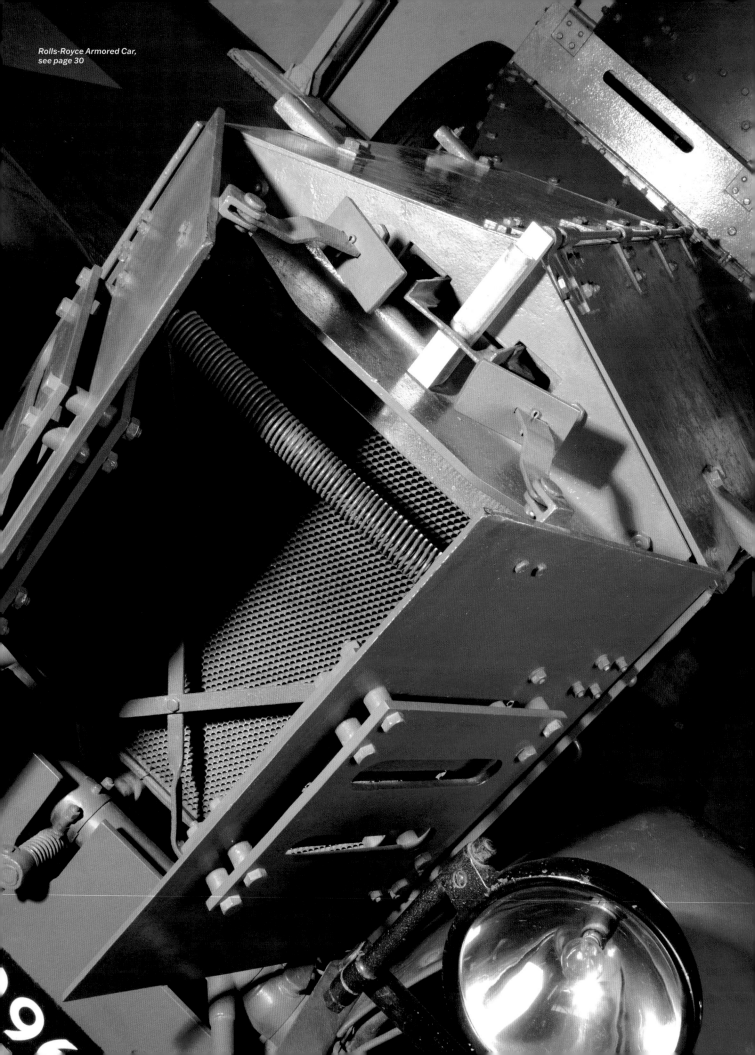

Rolls-Royce Armored Car,
see page 30